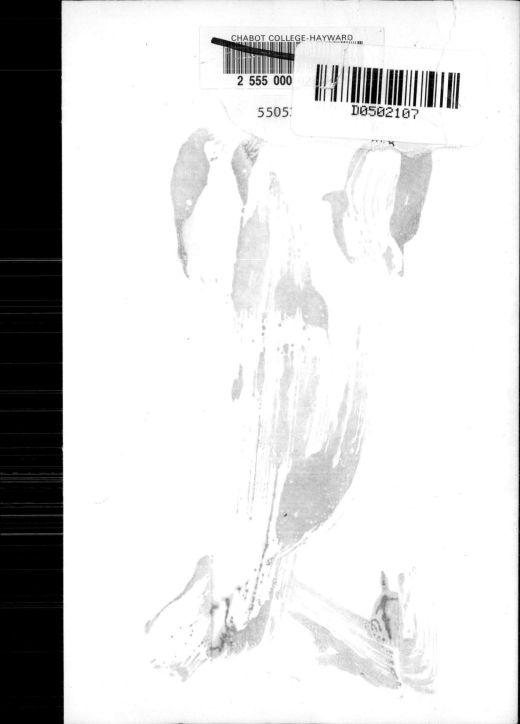

COPLAND ON MUSIC

AARON COPLAND was born in Brooklyn, N. Y., in 1900. He is one of the most frequently performed of American composers. As a member of many organizations, he has played an important role in the development of American music since the 1920s.

Copland's major works include the Piano Variations (1930), the ballet *Appalachian Spring* (1944), and the Third Symphony (1946). He has also composed chamber and choral music, film music, and an opera. His writings include three books—*What to Listen for in Music* (1939), *Our New Music* (1941), and *Music and Imagination* (1952)—in addition to the present one.

COPLAND ON MUSIC

by Aaron Copland

The Norton Library

W · W · NORTON & COMPANY · INC ·

NEW YORK

ML
63
C48

W. W. Norton & Company, Inc. is the publisher of current
or forthcoming books on music by Gerald Abraham, William Austin,
Anthony Baines, Sol Berkowitz, Friedrich Blume, Howard Boat-
wright, Nadia Boulanger, Nathan Broder, Manfred Bukofzer, John
Castellini, John Clough, Doda Conrad, Aaron Copland, Hans David,
Paul Des Marais, Otto Erich Deutsch, Frederick Dorian, Alfred
Einstein, Gabriel Fontrier, Karl Geiringer, Harold Gleason, Richard
Franko Goldman, Peter Gradenwitz, Donald Jay Grout, F. L.
Harrison, A. J. B. Hutchings, Charles Ives, Leo Kraft, Paul Henry
Lang, Jens Peter Larsen, Maurice Lieberman, Joseph Machlis, W. T.
Marrocco, Arthur Mendel, William J. Mitchell, Douglas Moore,
Carl Parrish, John F. Ohl, Vincent Persichetti, Marc Pincherle,
Walter Piston, Gustave Reese, Curt Sachs, Adolfo Salazar, Arnold
Schoenberg, Denis Stevens, Oliver Strunk, Francis Toye, Donald R.
Wakeling, Bruno Walter, and J. A. Westrup.

ACKNOWLEDGMENTS

I wish to make grateful acknowledgment to persons and publications who have given me the right to use material first published by them:

The Curtis Publishing Company, Philadelphia, Pa. for "The Pleasures of Music," published in part in *The Saturday Evening Post*, July 4, 1959, copyright © 1959 by The Curtis Publishing Company.

The American Academy of Arts and Letters, New York, N.Y., for *Creativity in America*, published in proceedings of the American Academy of Arts and Letters and the National Institute of Arts and Letters, Second Series, No. 3.

The Columbia University Press, New York, N.Y., for "Music as an Aspect of the Human Spirit," published in *Man's Right to Knowledge*, Second Series.

7

G. Schirmer, Inc., New York, N.Y., for "Serge Koussevitzky and the American Composer," published in the *Musical Quarterly* Vol. XXX, No. 3, July 1944; and "Current Chronicle" (William Schuman), published in the *Musical Quarterly*, New York, N.Y., Vol. 37, No. 3, July 1951.

Ballet Society, Inc., New York, N.Y., and Lincoln Kirstein, president, for "Influence, Problem, Tone," published in *Stravinsky in the Theatre*, copyright 1949 by Dance Index-Ballet Caravan, Inc.

Merle Armitage, Yucca Valley, California for "The Personality of Stravinsky," from the Merle Armitage book, *Stravinsky*, copyright 1949 by Merle Armitage, published by Duell, Sloane & Pearce, Inc.

The Music Library Association, Washington, D.C., for "Memorial to Paul Rosenfeld" and for "Benjamin Britten: The Rape of Lucretia," both published in *Notes*, Second Series, Vol. IV, No. 2, March 1947, copyright 1947 by Music Library Association, Inc.; and for "Stefan Wolpe: Two Songs for Alto and Piano, published in *Notes*, Second Series, Vol. VI, No. 1, December 1948, copyright 1948 by Music Library Association, Inc.; and "Leon Kirchner: Duo for violin and piano," published in *Notes*, Second Series, Vol. VII, No. 3, June 1950, copyright 1950, by Music Library Association, Inc.

The Billboard Publishing Co. (formerly Audiocom, Inc.), Great Barrington, Mass. for "At the Thought of Mozart," published in *High Fidelity*, January 1956.

The New York Times Company, New York, N.Y., for the following articles: "Faure Festival at Harvard," the New York *Times*, November 25, 1945; "The New School of American Composers," The New York *Times Magazine*, March 14, 1948; "The World of Atonality," The New York *Times Book Review*, November 27, 1949; "The Life and Music of Béla Bartók," The New York *Times Book Review*, May 3, 1953; "Modern Music: Fresh and Different," The New York *Times Magazine*, March 13, 1955.

The *Musical Courier*, New York, N.Y., for "The Dilemma of our Symphony Orchestras," published November 1, 1956, copyright 1956 by Gainsburg-Shack, Inc.

The Interstate Broadcasting Company, New York, N.Y., for "Latin Americans in Music," published in the WQXR *Program Guide*, June 1942.

The League of Composers, Inc., New York, N.Y., and Minna Lederman, former editor for publication in *Modern Music* of the following articles: "America's Young Men of Promise," Vol. III, No. 3, March–April 1926, copyright 1926 by The League of Composers, Inc.; "America's Young Men—Ten Years Later," Vol. XIII, No. 4, May 1936, copyright 1936 by The League of Composers, Inc.; "Playing Safe at Zurich," Vol. IV, No. 1, November–December 1926, copyright 1926 by The League of Composers, Inc.; "Baden-Baden," Vol. V, No. 1, November–December 1927, copyright 1927 by The League of Composers, Inc.; "Contemporaries at Oxford," Vol. VIII, No. 1, November–December 1930, copyright 1930 by The League of Composers, Inc.; "Stravinsky and Hindemith Premières," Vol. IX, No. 2, January–February 1932, copyright 1932 by The League of Composers, Inc.; "Thomson's Musical State," Vol. XVII, No. 1, October–November 1939, copyright 1939 by The League of Composers, Inc.; "The Composers of South America," Vol. XIX, No. 2, January 1942, copyright 1942 by The League of Composers, Inc.; "On the Notation of Rhythms," Vol. XXI, No. 4, May 1944, copyright 1944 by The League of Composers, Inc.

The *Saturday Review of Literature*, New York, N.Y., for "The Measure of Kapell," published November 28, 1953.

The *New Republic*, Washington, D.C., for "Stravinsky's Oedipus Rex," published February 29, 1928.

The *Sunday Times*, London, England, for "Interpreters and New Music," published October 12, 1958.

To my dear friend
HAROLD CLURMAN

CONTENTS

THIS BOOK CONTAINS a selection of occasional pieces about music and musicians written over a span of more than thirty years. Since many of them appeared in magazines and newspapers that are not easily accessible it is only natural that I should wish to make them available in more permanent form. Included also are some few articles printed here for the first time. Reading them together should help to make more evident one composer's viewpoint.

The opening section of the book concerns itself with thoughts about music as an art and with my enthusiasms for certain composers and musicians. The last section touches upon different phases of that perennial problem: contemporary music. In the central section I included a liberal number of how-it-seemed-then chapters, culled mostly from the musical scene of the twenties and thirties. Composers, unlike their literary counterparts in America, have only the slimmest of links with their own past. By recapturing some of the excitement of those earlier days in the immediacy of impressions and reactions set down then I hope to have stimulated the curiosity of readers younger than myself in their own musical background.

Needless to say, I revised no judgments in the light of later knowledge; to have done so would have been inconsistent with my purpose. (I did, however, shorten an article here and there in the interest of concision.) The reader should beware, therefore, of taking opinions expressed years ago, many of them based on incomplete evidence, as coinciding precisely with what I hold today. My hope is that these early evaluations may, at the very least, supply a modicum of historical perspective to those who imagine, as I was prone to do, that musical history begins with ourselves.

London, April 1960.

AUTHOR'S NOTE

IN PREPARING THIS volume for publication I had the valuable advice of my fellow-composer, Mr. Ychudi Wyner, to whom I wish to express my gratitude. I wish also to express appreciation to the editors and owners of various publications who assigned to me copyrights in the materials reprinted here: The National Academy of Arts and Letters, the Trustees of Columbia University, the New York *Times*, the *Saturday Review of Literature*, the *Musical Quarterly*, *High Fidelity* magazine, the *New Republic*, the London *Sunday Times*, and the WQXR *Program Guide*.

I wish especially to record my thankfulness to my friend of many years' standing, Minna Lederman Daniel, editor of the League of Composers' magazine, *Modern Music*, who not only allowed generous quotation from the pages of that publication, but in many instances instigated the writing of the sections in the first place.

Permission to reprint articles was also accorded by Richard Hill, of the Music Library Association, Merle

Author's Note

Armitage, Lincoln Kirstein, the Curtis Publishing Company, and Gainsburg-Shack, Inc., owners of the *Musical Courier*, to all of whom I owe thanks. Finally, I am grateful to David Walker for preparing the typescript for publication.

SECTION ONE

1. THREE TALKS

The Pleasures of Music *

PERHAPS I HAD BETTER begin by explaining that I think of myself as a composer of music and not as a writer about music. This distinction may not seem important to you, especially when I admit to having published several books on the subject. But to me the distinction is paramount because I know that if I were a writer I would be bubbling over with word-ideas about the art I practice, instead of which my mind—and not my mind only but my whole physical being vibrates to the stimulus of sound waves produced by instruments sounding alone or together. Why this is so I cannot tell you, but I can assure you it is so. Remembering then that I am primarily a composer and not a writer, I shall examine my subject mostly from the composer's standpoint in

* Delivered in the Distinguished Lecture Series at the University of New Hampshire in April 1959.

order to share with others, in so far as that is possible, the varied pleasures to be derived from experiencing music as an art.

That music gives pleasure is axiomatic. Because that is so, the pleasures of music as a subject for discussion may seem to some of you a rather elementary dish to place before so knowing an audience. But I think you will agree that the source of that pleasure, our musical instinct, is not at all elementary; it is, in fact, one of the prime puzzles of consciousness. Why is it that sound waves, when they strike the ear, cause "volleys of nerve impulses to flow up into the brain," resulting in a pleasurable sensation? More than that, why is it that we are able to make sense out of these "volleys of nerve signals" so that we emerge from engulfment in the orderly presentation of sound stimuli as if we had lived through a simulacrum of life, the instinctive life of the emotions? And why, when safely seated and merely listening, should our hearts beat faster, our temperature rise, our toes start tapping, our minds start racing after the music, hoping it will go one way and watching it go another, deceived and disgruntled when we are unconvinced, elated and grateful when we acquiesce?

We have a part answer, I suppose, in that the physical nature of sound has been thoroughly explored; but the phenomenon of music as an expressive, communicative agency remains as inexplicable as ever it was. We musicians don't ask for much. All we want is to have one investigator tell us why this young fellow seated in Row

A is firmly held by the musical sounds he hears while his girl friend gets little or nothing out of them, or vice versa. Think how many millions of useless practice hours might have been saved if some alert professor of genetics had developed a test for musical sensibility. The fascination of music for some human beings was curiously illustrated for me once during a visit I made to the showrooms of a manufacturer of electronic organs. As part of my tour I was taken to see the practice room. There, to my surprise, I found not one but eight aspiring organists, all busily practicing simultaneously on eight organs. More surprising still was the fact that not a sound was audible, for each of the eight performers was listening through earphones to his individual instrument. It was an uncanny sight, even for a fellow musician, to watch these grown men mesmerized, as it were, by a silent and invisible genie. On that day I fully realized how mesmerized we ear-minded creatures must seem to our less musically inclined friends.

If music has impact for the mere listener, it follows that it will have much greater impact for those who sing it or play it themselves with some degree of proficiency. Any educated person in Elizabethan times was expected to be able to read musical notation and take his or her part in a madrigal-sing. Passive listeners, numbered in the millions, are a comparatively recent innovation. Even in my own youth, loving music meant that you either made it yourself or were forced out of the house to go hear it where it was being made, at considerable cost and some

2 5

inconvenience. Nowadays all that has changed. Music has become so very accessible it is almost impossible to avoid it. Perhaps you don't mind cashing a check at the local bank to the strains of a Brahms symphony, but I do. Actually, I think I spend as much time avoiding great works as others spend in seeking them out. The reason is simple: meaningful music demands one's undivided attention, and I can give it that only when I am in a receptive mood, and feel the need for it. The use of music as a kind of ambrosia to titillate the aural senses while one's conscious mind is otherwise occupied is the abomination of every composer who takes his work seriously.

Thus, the music I have reference to in this article is designed for your undistracted attention. It is, in fact, usually labeled "serious" music in contradistinction to light or popular music. How this term "serious" came into being no one seems to know, but all of us are agreed as to its inadequacy. It just doesn't cover enough cases. Very often our "serious" music *is* serious, sometimes deadly serious, but it can also be witty, humorous, sarcastic, sardonic, grotesque and a great many other things besides. It is, indeed, the emotional range covered that makes it "serious" and, in part, influences our judgment as to the artistic stature of any extended composition.

Everyone is aware that so-called serious music has made great strides in general public acceptance in recent years, but the term itself still connotes something forbidding and hermetic to the mass audience. They attribute to the professional musician a kind of Masonic initiation into secrets that are forever hidden from the outsider. Nothing could be more misleading. We all listen to music, professionals and non-professionals alike, in the same sort of way—in a dumb sort of way, really, because simple or sophisticated music attracts all of us, in the first instance, on the primordial level of sheer rhythmic and sonic appeal. Musicians are flattered, no doubt, by the deferential attitude of the layman in regard to what he imagines to be our secret understanding of music. But in all honesty we musicians know that in the main we listen basically as others do, because music hits us with an immediacy that we recognize in the reactions of the most simple-minded of music listeners.

It is part of my thesis that music, unlike the other arts, with the possible exception of dancing, gives pleasure simultaneously on the lowest and highest levels of apprehension. All of us, for example, can understand and feel the joy of being carried forward by the flow of music. Our love of music is bound up with its forward motion; nonetheless it is precisely the creation of that sense of flow, its interrelation with and resultant effect upon formal structure, that calls forth high intellectual capacities of a composer, and offers keen pleasures for listening minds. Music's incessant movement forward exerts a double and contradictory fascination: on the one hand it appears to be immobilizing time itself by filling out a specific temporal space, while generating at the same moment the sensation of flowing past us with all the pressure and sparkle of a great river. To stop the flow of music would be like the stopping of time itself, incredible and inconceivable. Only a catastrophe of some sort produces such a break in the musical discourse during a public performance. Musicians are, of course, hardened to such interruptions during rehearsal periods, but they don't relish them. The public, at such times, look on, unbelieving. I have seen this demonstrated each summer at Tanglewood during the open rehearsals of the Boston Symphony Orchestra. Large audiences gather each week, I am convinced, for the sole pleasure of living through that awefull moment when the conductor abruptly stops the music. Something went wrong; no one seems to know what or why, but it stopped the music's flow, and a shock of recognition runs through the entire crowd. That is what they came for, though they may not realize it—that, and the pleasure of hearing the music's flow resumed, which lights up the public countenance with a kind of all's-right-with-the-world assurance. Clearly, audience enjoyment is inherent in the magnetic forward pull of the music; but to the more enlightened listener this time-filling, forward drive has fullest meaning only when accompanied by some conception as to where it is heading, what musical-psychological elements are helping to move it to its destination, and what formal architectural satisfactions will have been achieved on its arriving there.

Musical flow is largely the result of musical rhythm, and the rhythmic factor in music is certainly a key element that has simultaneous attraction on more than one level. To some African tribes rhythm *is* music; they have nothing more. But what rhythm it is! Listening to it casually, one might never get beyond the earsplitting poundings, but actually a trained musician's ear is needed to disengage its polyrhythmic intricacies. Minds that conceive such rhythms have their own sophistication; it seems inexact and even unfair to call them primitive. By comparison our own instinct for rhythmic play seems only mild in interest—needing reinvigoration from time to time.

It was because the ebb of rhythmic invention was comparatively low in late-nineteenth-century European music that Stravinsky was able to apply what I once termed "a rhythmic hypodermic" to Western music. His shocker of 1913, *The Rite of Spring,* a veritable rhythmic monstrosity to its first hearers, has now become a standard item of the concert repertory. This indicates the progress that has been made in the comprehension and enjoyment of rhythmic complexities that nonplused our grand-fathers. And the end is by no means in sight. Younger composers have taken us to the very limit of what the human hand can perform and have gone even beyond what the human ear can grasp in rhythmic differentiation. Sad to say, there is a limit, dictated by what nature has supplied us with in the way of listening equipment. But within those limits there are large areas of rhythmic life still to be explored, rhythmic forms never dreamed of by composers of the march or the mazurka.

In so saying I do not mean to minimize the rhythmic ingenuities of past eras. The wonderfully subtle rhythms of the anonymous composers of the late fourteenth century, only recently deciphered; the delicate shadings of oriental rhythms; the carefully contrived speech-based rhythms of the composers of Tudor England; and, bringing things closer to home, the improvised wildness of jazz-inspired rhythms—all these and many more must be rated, certainly, as prime musical pleasures.

Tone color is another basic element in music that may be enjoyed on various levels of perception from the most naïve to the most cultivated. Even children have no difficulty in recognizing the difference between the tonal profile of a flute and a trombone. The color of certain instruments holds an especial attraction for certain people. I myself have always had a weakness for the sound of eight French horns playing in unison. Their rich, golden, legendary sonority transports me. Some present-day European composers seem to be having a belated love affair with the vibraphone. An infinitude of possible color combinations is available when instruments are mixed, especially when combined in that wonderful contraption, the orchestra of symphonic proportions. The art of orchestration, needless to say, holds endless fascination for the practicing composer, being part science and part inspired guesswork.

As a composer I get great pleasure from cooking up tonal combinations. Over the years I have noted that no element of the composer's art mystifies the layman more than this ability to conceive mixed instrumental colors. But remember that before we mix them we hear them in terms of their component parts. If you examine an orchestral score you will note that composers place their instruments on the page in family groups: in reading from top to bottom it is customary to list the woodwinds, the brass, the percussion, and the strings, in that order. Modern orchestral practice often juxtaposes these families one against the other so that their personalities, as families, remain recognizable and distinct. This principle may also be applied to the voice of the single instrument, whose pure color sonority thereby remains clearly identifiable as such. Orchestral know-how consists in keeping the instruments out of each other's way, so spacing them that they avoid repeating what some other instrument is already doing, at least in the same register, thereby exploiting to the fullest extent the specific color value contributed by each separate instrument or grouped instrumental family.

In modern orchestration clarity and definition of sonorous image are usually the goal. There exists, however, another kind of orchestral magic dependent on a certain ambiguity of effect. Not to be able to identify immediately how a particular color combination is arrived at adds to its attractiveness. I like to be intrigued by unusual sounds that force me to exclaim: Now I wonder how the composer does that?

From what I have said about the art of orchestration you may have gained the notion that it is nothing more than a delightful game, played for the amusement of the composer. That is, of course, not true. Color in music, as in painting, is meaningful only when it serves the expressive idea; it is the expressive idea that dictates to the composer the choice of his orchestral scheme.

Part of the pleasure in being sensitive to the use of color in music is to note in what way a composer's personality traits are revealed through his tonal color schemes. During the period of French impressionism, for example, the composers Debussy and Ravel were thought to be very similar in personality. An examination of their orchestral scores would have shown that Debussy, at his most characteristic, sought for a spray-like iridescence, a delicate and sensuous sonority such as had never before been heard, while Ravel, using a similar palette, sought a refinement and precision, a gemlike brilliance that reflects the more objective nature of his musical personality.

Color ideals change for composers as their personalities change. A striking example is again that of Igor Stravinsky, who, beginning with the stabbing reds and purples of his early ballet scores, has in the past decade arrived at an ascetic grayness of tone that positively chills the listener by its austerity. For contrast we may turn to a Richard Strauss orchestral score, masterfully handled in its own way, but overrich in the piling-on of sonorities, like a German meal that is too filling for comfort. The natural and easy handling of orchestral forces by a whole school of contemporary American composers would indicate some inborn affinity between American personality traits and symphonic language. No layman can hope to penetrate all the subtleties that go into an orchestral page of any complexity, but here again it is not necessary to be able to analyze the color spectrum of a score in order to bask in its effulgence.

Thus far I have been dealing with the generalities of musical pleasure. Now I wish to concentrate on the music of a few composers in order to show how musical values are differentiated. The late Serge Koussevitzky, conductor of the Boston Symphony, never tired of telling performers that if it weren't for composers they would literally have nothing to play or sing. He was stressing what is too often taken for granted and, therefore, lost sight of, namely, that in our Western world music speaks with a composer's voice and half the pleasure we get comes from the fact that we are listening to a particular voice making an individual statement at a specific moment in history. Unless you take off from there, you are certain to miss one of the principal attractions of musical art—contact with a strong and absorbing personality.

It matters greatly, therefore, who it is we are about to listen to in the concert hall or opera house. And yet I get the impression that to the lay music-lover music is music and musical events are attended with little or no concern as to what musical fare is to be offered. Not so with the professional, to whom it matters a great deal whether he is about to listen to the music of Monteverdi or Massenet, to J. S. or to J. C. Bach. Isn't it true that everything we, as listeners, know about a particular composer and his music prepares us in some measure to empathize with his special mentality? To me Chopin is one thing,

33

Scarlatti quite another. I could never confuse them, could you? Well, whether you could or not, my point remains the same: there are as many ways for music to be enjoyable as there are composers.

One can even get a certain perverse pleasure out of hating the work of a particular composer. I, for instance, happen to be rubbed the wrong way by one of today's composer-idols, Serge Rachmaninoff. The prospect of having to sit through one of his extended symphonies or piano concertos tends, quite frankly, to depress me. All those notes, think I, and to what end? To me Rachmaninoff's characteristic tone is one of self-pity and self-indulgence tinged with a definite melancholia. As a fellow human being I can sympathize with an artist whose distempers produced such music, but as a listener my stomach won't take it. I grant you his technical adroitness, but even here the technique adopted by the composer was old-fashioned in his own day. I also grant his ability to write long and singing melodic lines, but when these are embroidered with figuration, the musical substance is watered down, emptied of significance. Well, as André Gide used to say, I didn't have to tell you this, and I know it will not make you happy to hear it. Actually it should be of little concern to you whether I find Rachmaninoff digestible. All I am trying to say is that music strikes us in as many different ways as there are composers, and anything less than a strong reaction, pro or con, is not worth bothering about.

By contrast, let me point to that perennially popular

favorite among composers, Giuseppe Verdi. Quite apart from his music, I get pleasure merely thinking about the man himself. If honesty and forthrightness ever sparked an artist, then Verdi is a prime example. What a pleasure it is to make contact with him through his letters, to knock against the hard core of his peasant personality. One comes away refreshed, and with renewed confidence in the sturdy non-neurotic character of at least one musical master.

When I was a student it was considered not good form to mention Verdi's name in symphonic company, and quite out of the question to name Verdi in the same sentence with that formidable dragon of the opera house, Richard Wagner. What the musical elite found difficult to forgive in Verdi's case was his triteness, his ordinariness. Yes, Verdi is trite and ordinary at times, just as Wagner is long-winded and boring at times. There is a lesson to be learned here: the way in which we are gradually able to accommodate our minds to the obvious weaknesses in a creative artist's output. Musical history teaches us that at first contact the academicisms of Brahms, the *longueurs* of Schubert, the portentousness of Mahler were considered insupportable by their early listeners—but in all such cases later generations have managed to put up with the failings of men of genius for the sake of other qualities that outweigh them.

Verdi can be commonplace at times, as everyone knows, but his saving grace is a burning sincerity that carries all before it. There is no bluff here, no guile. On whatever level he composed a no-nonsense quality comes across; all is directly stated, cleanly written with no notes wasted, and marvelously effective. In the end we willingly concede that Verdi's musical materials need not be especially choice in order to be acceptable. And, naturally enough, when the musical materials *are* choice and inspired, they profit doubly from being set off against the homely virtues of his more workaday pages.

Verdi's creative life lasted for more than half a century, advancing steadily in musical interest and sophistication. So prolonged a capacity for development has few parallels in musical annals. There is a special joy in following the milestones of a career that began so modestly and obscurely, leading gradually to the world renown of *Traviata* and *Aïda*, and then, to the general astonishment of the musical community, continuing on in the eighth decade of his life to the crowning achievements of *Otello* and *Falstaff*.

If one were asked to name one musician who came closest to composing without human flaw I suppose general concensus would choose Johann Sebastian Bach. Only a very few musical giants have earned the universal admiration that surrounds the figure of this eighteenth-century German master. America should love Bach, for he is the greatest, as we would say—or, if not the greatest, he has few rivals and no peers. What is it, then, that makes his finest scores so profoundly moving? I have puzzled over that question for a very long time, but have come to doubt whether it is possible for anyone to reach a completely satisfactory answer. One thing is certain; we will never explain Bach's supremacy by the singling out of any one element in his work. Rather it was a combination of perfections, each of which was applied to the common practice of his day; added together, they produced the mature perfection of the completed *oeuvre*.

Bach's genius cannot possibly be deduced from the circumstances of his routine musical existence. All his life long he wrote music for the requirements of the jobs he held. His melodies were often borrowed from liturgical sources, his orchestral textures limited by the forces at his disposal, and his forms, in the main, were similar to those of other composers of his time, whose works, incidentally, he had closely studied. To his more up-to-date composer sons Father Bach was, first of all, a famous instrumental performer, and only secondarily a solid craftsman-creator of the old school, whose compositions were little known abroad for the simple reason that few of them were published in his lifetime. None of these oft-repeated facts explains the universal hold his best music has come to have on later generations.

What strikes me most markedly about Bach's work is the marvelous rightness of it. It is the rightness not merely of a single individual but of a whole musical epoch. Bach came at the peak point of a long historical development; his was the heritage of many generations of composing artisans. Never since that time has music so successfully fused contrapuntal skill with harmonic logic. This amalgam of melodies and chords—of independent lines con-

37

ceived linear-fashion within a mold of basic harmonies conceived vertically—provided Bach with the necessary framework for his massive edifice. Within that edifice is the summation of an entire period, with all the grandeur, nobility, and inner depth that one creative soul could bring to it. It is hopeless, I fear, to attempt to probe further into why his music creates the impression of spiritual wholeness, the sense of his communing with the deepest vision. We would only find ourselves groping for words, words that can never hope to encompass the intangible greatness of music, least of all the intangible in Bach's greatness.

Those who are interested in studying the interrelationship between a composer and his work would do better to turn to the century that followed Bach's, and especially to the life and work of Ludwig van Beethoven. The English critic, Wilfrid Mellers, had this to say about Beethoven, recently: "It is the essence of the personality of Beethoven, both as man and as artist, that he should invite discussion in other than musical terms." Mellers meant that such a discussion would involve us, with no trouble at all, in a consideration of the rights of man, free will, Napoleon and the French Revolution, and other allied subjects. We shall never know in exactly what way the ferment of historical events affected Beethoven's thinking, but it is certain that music such as his would have been inconceivable in the early nineteenth century without serious concern for the revolutionary temper of his time and the ability to translate that concern into the original and unprecedented musical thought of his own work.

Beethoven brought three startling innovations to music: first, he altered our very conception of the art by emphasizing the psychological element implicit in the language of sounds. Because of him, music lost a certain innocence but gained instead a new dimension in psychological depth. Secondly, his own stormy and explosive temperament was, in part, responsible for a "dramatization of the whole art of music." The rumbling bass tremolandos, the sudden accents in unexpected places, the hitherto-unheard-of rhythmic insistence and sharp dynamic contrasts—all these were externalizations of an inner drama that gave his music theatrical impact. Both these elements—the psychological orientation and the instinct for drama—are inextricably linked in my mind with his third and possibly most original achievement: the creation of musical forms dynamically conceived on a scale never before attempted and of an inevitability that is irresistible. Especially the sense of inevitability is remarkable in Beethoven. Notes are not words, they are not under the control of verifiable logic, and because of that composers in every age have struggled to overcome that handicap by producing a directional effect convincing to the listeners. No composer has ever solved the problem more brilliantly than Beethoven; nothing quite so inevitable had ever before been created in the language of sounds.

One doesn't need much historical perspective to

realize what a shocking experience Beethoven's music must have been for his first listeners. Even today, given the nature of his music, there are times when I simply do not understand how this man's art was "sold" to the big musical public. Obviously he must be saying something that everyone wants to hear. And yet if one listens freshly and closely the odds against acceptance are equally obvious. As sheer sound there is little that is luscious about his music—it gives off a comparatively "dry" sonority. He never seems to flatter an audience, never to know or care what they might like. His themes are not particularly lovely or memorable; they are more likely to be expressively apt than beautifully contoured. His general manner is gruff and unceremonious, as if the matter under discussion were much too important to be broached in urbane or diplomatic terms. He adopts a peremptory and hortatory tone, the assumption being, especially in his most forceful work, that you have no choice but to listen. And that is precisely what happens: you listen. Above and beyond every other consideration Beethoven has one quality to a remarkable degree: he is enormously compelling.

What is it he is so compelling about? How can one not be compelled and not be moved by the moral fervor and conviction of such a man? His finest works are the enactment of a triumph—a triumph of affirmation in the face of the human condition. Beethoven is one of the great yea-sayers among creative artists; it is exhilarating to share his clear-eyed contemplation of the tragic sum of life. His music summons forth our better nature; in purely musical terms Beethoven seems to be exhorting us to Be Noble, Be Strong, Be Great in Heart, yes, and Be Compassionate. These ethical precepts we subsume from the music, but it is the music itself—the nine symphonies, the sixteen string quartets, the thirty-two piano sonatas—that holds us, and holds us in much the same way each time we return to it. The core of Beethoven's music seems indestructible; the ephemera of sound seem to have little to do with its strangely immutable substance.

What a contrast it is to turn from the starkness of Beethoven to the very different world of a composer like Palestrina. Palestrina's music is heard more rarely than that of the German master; possibly because of that it seems more special and remote. In Palestrina's time it was choral music that held the center of the stage, and many composers lived their lives, as did Palestrina, attached to the service of the Church. Without knowing the details of his life story, and from the evidence of the music alone, it is clear that the purity and serenity of his work reflects a profound inner peace. Whatever the stress and strain of daily living in sixteenth-century Rome may have been, his music breathes quietly in some place apart. Everything about it conduces to the contemplative life: the sweetness of the modal harmonies, the stepwise motion of the melodic phrases, the consummate ease in the handling of vocal polyphony. His music looks white upon the page and sounds "white" in the voices. Its homogeneity of style, composed, as much of it was, for ecclesiastical devotions, gives it a pervading mood of impassivity and other-worldliness. Such music, when it is merely routine, can be pale and dull. But at its best Palestrina's masses and motets create an ethereal loveliness that only the world of tones can embody.

My concern here with composers of the first rank like Bach and Beethoven and Palestrina is not meant to suggest that only the greatest names and the greatest masterpieces are worth your attention. Musical art, as we hear it in our day, suffers if anything from an overdose of masterworks, an obsessive fixation on the glories of the past. This narrows the range of our musical experience and tends to suffocate interest in the present. It blots out many an excellent composer whose work was less than perfect. I cannot agree, for instance, with Albert Schweitzer, who once remarked that "of all arts music is that in which perfection is a *sine qua non*, and that the predecessors of Bach were foredoomed to comparative oblivion because their works were not mature." It may be carping to say so, but the fact is that we tire of everything, even of perfection. It would be truer to point out, it seems to me, that the forerunners of Bach have an awkward charm and simple grace that not even he could match, just because of his mature perfection. Delacroix had something of my idea when he complained in his journal about Racine being too perfect: that "that perfection and the absence of breaks and incongruities deprive him of the spice one finds in works full of beauties and defects at the same time."

Our musical pleasures have been largely extended in recent years by familiarity (often through recordings), with a period of musical history, "full of beauties and defects," that long antedates the era of Bach. Musicologists, sometimes reproached for their pedanticism, have in this case put before us musical delicacies revived out of what appeared to be an unrecoverable past. Pioneering groups in more than one musical center have revivified a whole musical epoch by deciphering early manuscripts of anonymous composers, reconstructing obsolete instruments, imagining, as best they can, what may have been the characteristic vocal sound in that far-off time. Out of scholarly research and a fair amount of plain conjecture they have made it possible for us to hear music of an extraordinary sadness and loneliness, with a textural bareness that reminds us at times of the work of some present-day composers. This is contrasted with dancelike pieces that are touching in their innocence. The naïveté of this music—or what seems to us naïve—has encouraged a polite approach to the problems of actual performance that I find hard to connect with the more rugged aspects of the Middle Ages. But no matter; notions as to interpretation will change and in the meantime we have learned to stretch the conventional limits of usable musical history and draw upon a further storehouse of musical treasures.

A young American poet wrote recently: "We cannot know anything about the past unless we know about the present." Part of the pleasure of involving oneself with the

43

arts is the excitement of venturing out among its contemporary manifestations. But a strange thing happens in this connection in the field of music. The same people who find it quite natural that modern books, plays, or paintings are likely to be controversial seem to want to escape being challenged and troubled when they turn to music. In our field there appears to be a never-ending thirst for the familiar, and very little curiosity as to what the newer composers are up to. Such music-lovers, as I see it, simply don't love music enough, for if they did their minds would not be closed to an area that holds the promise of fresh and unusual musical experience. Charles Ives used to say that people who couldn't put up with dissonance in music had "sissy ears." Fortunately there are in all countries today some braver souls who mind not at all having to dig a bit for their musical pleasure, who actually enjoy being confronted with the creative artist who is problematical.

Paul Valéry tells us that in France it was Stéphane Mallarmé who became identified in the public mind as the prototype of difficult author. It was his poetry, according to Valéry, that engendered a new species of reader, who, as Valéry puts it, "couldn't conceive of *plaisir sans peine* [pleasure without trouble], who didn't like to enjoy himself without paying for it, and who even couldn't feel happy unless his joy was in some measure the result of his own work, wishing to feel what his own effort cost him . . ." This passage is exactly applicable to certain lovers of contemporary music. They refuse to be frightened off too easily. I myself, when I encounter a piece of music whose import escapes me immediately, think: "*I'm not getting this. I shall have to come back to it for a second or third try.*" I don't at all mind actively disliking a piece of contemporary music, but in order to feel happy about it I must consciously understand why I dislike it. Otherwise it remains in my mind as unfinished business.

This doesn't resolve the problem of the music-lover of good will who says: "I'd like to like this modern stuff, but what do I do?" Well, the unvarnished truth is that there are no magic formulas, no short cuts for making the unfamiliar seem comfortably familiar. There is no advice one can give other than to say: relax—that's of first importance—and then listen to the same pieces enough times to really matter. Fortunately not all new music must be rated as difficult to comprehend. I once had occasion to divide contemporary composers into categories of relative difficulty from very easy to very tough, and a surprising number of composers fitted into the first group. Of the problematical composers it is the practitioners of twelve-tone music who are the hardest to comprehend because their abandonment of tonality constitutes a body blow to age-old listening habits. No other phase of the new in music—not the violence of expression, nor the dissonant counterpoint, nor the unusual forms—has offered the stumbling block of the loss of a centered tonality. What Arnold Schönberg began in the first decade of this century, moving from his tonally liberated early pieces to his fully integrated twelve-tone compositions, has

45

shaken the very foundations of musical art. No wonder it is still in the process of being gradually absorbed and digested.

The question that wants answering is whether Schönberg's twelve-tone music is the way to the future or whether it is merely a passing phase. Unfortunately it must remain an open question, for there are no guaranteed prognostications in the arts. All we know is that so-called difficult composers have sometimes been the subject of remarkable revisions of opinion. One recent example is the case of Béla Bartók. None of us who knew his music at the time of his death in 1945 could have predicted the sudden upsurge of interest in his work and its present world-wide dissemination. One would have thought his musical speech too dour, too insistent, too brittle and uncompromising to hold the attention of the widest audience. And yet we were proved wrong. Conductors and performers seized upon his work at what must have been the right moment, a moment when the big public was ready for his kind of rhythmic vitality, his passionate and despairing lyricism, his superb organizational gift that rounds out the over-all shape of a movement while keeping every smallest detail relevant to the main discourse. Whatever the reasons, the Bartók case proves that there is an unconscious evolutionary process at work, responsible for sudden awareness and understanding in our listening habits.

One of the attractions of concerning oneself with the new in music is the possible discovery of important work

by the younger generation of composers. Certain patrons
of music, certain publishers and conductors, and more
rarely some older composers have shown a special pen-
chant for what the younger generation is up to. Franz
Liszt, for instance, was especially perceptive in sensing the
mature composer while still in the embryonic stage. In his
own day he was in touch with and encouraged the nationalist strivings of young composers like Grieg, Smetana,
Borodine, Albéniz, and our own Edward MacDowell. The
French critic Sainte-Beuve, writing at about that period,
had this to say about discovering young talent: "I know
of no pleasure more satisfying for the critic than to understand and describe a young talent in all its freshness, its
open and primitive quality, before it is glossed over later
by whatever is acquired and perhaps manufactured."

Today's typical young men appeared on the scene in
the postwar years. They upset their elders in the traditional way by positing a new ideal for music. This time
they called for a music that was to be thoroughly controlled in its every particular. As hero they chose a pupil
and disciple of Schönberg, Anton Webern, whose later
music was in many ways a more logical and less romantic
application of Schönbergian twelve-tone principles. Inspired by Webern's curiously original and seldom-per-
formed music, every element of musical composition was
now to be put under rigorous control. Not only the tone
rows and their resultant harmonies, but even rhythms and
dynamics were to be given the dodecaphonic treatment.
The music they produced, admirably logical on paper,

makes a rather haphazard impression in actual performance. I very well remember my first reactions on hearing
examples of the latest music of these young men, because
I noted them at the time. Let me read you a brief excerpt:
"One gets the notion that these boys are starting again
from the beginning, with the separate tone and the separate sonority. Notes are strewn about like *disjecta membra;*
there is an end to continuity in the old sense and an end of
thematic relationships. In this music one waits to hear
what will happen next without the slightest idea what *will*
happen, or why what happened did happen once it has
happened. Perhaps one can say modern painting of the
Paul Klee school has invaded the new music. The so-to-
speak disrelation of unrelated tones is the way I might
describe it. No one really knows where it will go, and
neither do I. One thing is sure, however, whatever the
listener may think of it, it is without doubt the most
frustrating music ever put on a performer's music-stand."

Since I made those notations some of the younger
European composers have branched off into the first tentative experiments with electronically produced music.
No performers, no musical instruments, no microphones
are needed. But one must be able to record on tape and
be able to feed into it electromagnetic vibrations. Those
of you who have heard recordings of recent electronic
compositions will agree, I feel sure, that in this case we
shall have to broaden our conception of what is to be included under the heading of musical pleasure. It will
have to take into account areas of sound hitherto excluded

from the musical scheme of things. And why not? With
so many other of man's assumptions subject to review
how could one expect music to remain the same? Whatever we may think of their efforts, these young experiment-
ers obviously need more time; it is pointless to attempt
evaluations before they have more fully explored the new
terrain. A few names have come to the fore: in Germany,
Karlheinz Stockhausen, in France, Pierre Boulez, in Italy,
Luigi Nono and Luciano Berio. What they have composed
has produced polemics, publication, radio sponsorship
abroad, annual conclaves—but no riots. The violent reaction of the teens and twenties to the then-new music of
Stravinsky, Darius Milhaud, and Schönberg is, apparently,
not to be repeated so soon again. We have all learned
a thing or two about taking shocks, musical and otherwise. The shock may be gone but the challenge is still
there and if our love for music is as all-embracing as it
should be, we ought to want to meet it head on.

It hardly seems possible to conclude a talk on musical
pleasures at an American university without mentioning
that ritualistic word, jazz. But, someone is sure to ask, is
jazz serious? I'm afraid that it is too late to bother with the
question, since jazz, serious or not, is very much here, and
it obviously provides pleasure. The confusion comes, I
believe, from attempting to make the jazz idiom cover
broader expressive areas than naturally belong to it. Jazz
does *not* do what serious music does either in its range of
emotional expressivity or in its depth of feeling, nor in its
universality of language. (It does have universality of ap-

peal, which is not the same thing.) On the other hand, jazz does do what serious music cannot do, namely, suggest a colloquialism of musical speech that is indigenously delightful, a kind of here-and-now feeling, less enduring than classical music, perhaps, but with an immediacy and vibrancy that audiences throughout the world find exhilarating.

Personally I like my jazz free and untrammeled, as far removed from the regular commercial product as possible. Fortunately the more progressive jazz men seem to be less and less restrained by the conventionalities of their idiom, so little restrained that they appear in fact to be headed our way. By that I mean that harmonic and structural freedoms of recent serious music have had so considerable an influence on the younger jazz composers that it becomes increasingly difficult to keep the categories of jazz and non-jazz clearly divided. A new kind of crossfertilization of our two worlds is developing that promises an unusual synthesis for the future. We on the serious side greatly envy the virtuosity of the jazz instrumentalist, particularly his ability to improvise freely, and sometimes spectacularly apropos of a given theme. The jazz men, on their side, seem to be taking themselves with a new seriousness; to be exploring new instrumental combinations, daring harmonic patterns—going so far occasionally as to give up the famous jazz beat that keeps all its disparate elements together, and taking on formal problems far removed from the symmetrical regularities imposed on an earlier jazz. Altogether the scene is lively, very lively, and a very full half century away from the time when Debussy was inspired to write *Golliwog's Cake-walk*.

By now I hope to have said enough to have persuaded you of the largesse of musical pleasure that awaits the gifted listener. The art of music, without specific subject matter and with little specific meaning, is nonetheless a balm for the human spirit—not a refuge or escape from the realities of existence, but a haven wherein one makes contact with the essence of human experience. I myself take sustenance from music as one would from a spring. I invite you all to partake of that pleasure.

Creativity in America*

THE CREATIVE SPIRIT, as it manifests itself in our America, is assuredly an appropriate subject to bring before this academy and institute, dedicated as they are to the "furtherance of literature and the fine arts in the

* Presented as The Blashfield Address before The American Academy and National Institute of Arts and Letters, May 1952.

United States." We here know that the creative act is central to the life process. The creative act goes far back in time; it has functioned and continues to function in every human community and on every level of mankind's development, so that by now it possesses an almost hieratic significance—a significance akin to that of the religious experience. A civilization that produces no creative artists is either wholly provincial or wholly dead. A mature people senses the need to leave traces of its essential character in works of art, otherwise a powerful incentive is lacking in the will to live.

What, precisely, does creativity mean in the life of a man and of a nation? For one thing, the creative act affirms the individual, and gives value to the individual, and through him to the nation of which he is a part. The creative person makes evident his deepest experience— summarizes that experience and sets up a chain of communication with his fellow-man on a level far more profound than anything known to the workaday world. The experience of art cleanses the emotions; through it we touch the wildness of life, and its basic intractability; and through it we come closest to shaping an essentially intractable material into some degree of permanence and of beauty.

The man who lives the creative life in today's world is, in spite of himself, a symbolic figure. Wherever he may be or whatever he may say, he is in his own mind the embodiment of the free man. He must feel free in order to function creatively, for only in so far as he functions as he pleases will he create significant work. He must have the right to protest or even to revile his own time if he sees fit to do so, as well as the possibility of sounding its praises. Above all he must never give up the right to be wrong, for the creator must forever be instinctive and spontaneous in his impulses, which means that he may learn as much from his miscalculations as from his successful achievements. I am not suggesting that the artist is without restraint of any kind. But the artist's discipline is a mature discipline because it is self-imposed, acting as a stimulus to the creative mind.

Creative persons, when they gather together, seldom speak of these matters as I speak of them now. They take them for granted, for they are quite simply the "facts of life" to the practicing artist. Actually, the creator lives in a more intuitive world than the consciously ordered one that I have pictured here. He is aware not so much of the human and aesthetic implications of the rounded and finished work as he is of the imperfections of the work in progress. Paul Valéry used to say that an artist never finishes a work, he merely abandons it. But of course, when he abandons it, it is in order to begin anew with still another work. Thus the artist lives in a continual state of self-discovery, believing both in the value of his own work and in its perfectability. As a free man he sets an example of persistence and belief that other men would do well to ponder, especially in a world distracted and ridden with self-doubts.

All this is very probably elementary stuff to the mem-

53

bers of this distinguished community of creators. But the question in my mind is whether it is correct to assume that it is also "baby stuff" for the generality of our fellow citizens. Does the average American really grasp the concept included in the word "creativity"? Have the artists of America succeeded in impressing themselves—that is to say, in the deepest sense—on the mind of America? Frankly, I seriously doubt it. Some of my friends tell me that there are no special circumstances that surround the idea of creativity in our country, and that my theme—creativity in America—makes no sense, because creativity is the same everywhere. But my observation and experience convince me of two things: first, that the notion of the creative man plays a less important role here than is true in other countries; and second, that it is especially necessary that we, the artists of America, make clear to our countrymen the value attached in all lands to the idea of the creative personality.

The origins of the American attitude toward creativity are understandable enough. We are the heirs of a colonial people, and because for so long we imported cultural riches from overseas, it became traditional for Americans to think of art as something purchased abroad. Fortunately there are signs that the notion is slowly dissolving, probably forever, along with other nineteenth-century preconceptions about art in America. Europeans, however, seem intent upon perpetuating that myth. When I was abroad in 1951 I was aware of a certain reluctance on the part of the ordinary music-lover to believe that America might be capable of producing first-rate work in the field of music. The inference seemed to be that it was unfair for a country to have industrial and scientific power and, at the same time, the potentiality of developing cultural power also. At every opportunity I pointed out that it is just because commercial and scientific know-how alone are insufficient to justify a civilization that it is doubly necessary for countries like the United States to prove that it is possible, at the same time, to produce, along with men of commerce and of science, creative artists who can carry on the cultural tradition of mankind.

The British music critic Wilfrid Mellers dramatized the crucial role America must play in this regard by writing that "the creation of a vital American music [he might have written American poetry or American painting] . . . is inseparable from the continuance of civilization." One might, I suppose, use a less grandiose phrase and put it this way: to create a work of art in a non-industrial community and in an unsophisticated environment is comparatively unproblematical. Thus the impoverished peon with none of the distractions of modern urban life carves something out of a piece of wood, or weaves a design in cloth. Subsequently someone comes along and says: "Why, this is art; we must put it into a museum." A contrasted though analogous situation obtains in a country like France. There a long tradition of cultural achievement has been established for many centuries; hence it is not surprising that a young generation can carry that tradition forward through the creation of new works of art. Creativity in such an environment does not take *too* much imagination. But in a civilization like our own, with few traditional concepts, and with many conflicting drives, each generation must reaffirm the possibility of the coexistence of industrialism and creative activity. It is as if each creative artist had to reinvent the creative process for himself alone, and then venture forth to find an audience responsive enough to have some inkling of what he was up to in the first instance.

I say this with a certain amount of personal feeling, as a native from across the East River, who grew up in an environment that could hardly have been described as artistic. My discovery of music and the allied arts was the natural unfolding of an inner compulsion. I realize that not all lovers of art can be expected to have the kind of immediacy of contact that is typical of the practicing artist. What seems important to me is not that all our citizens understand art in general, or even the art that we ourselves make, but that they become fully cognizant of the civilizing force that the work of art represents— a civilizing force that is urgently needed in our time. My fear is not that art will be crushed in America, but that it won't be noticed sufficiently to matter.

Whose fault is it that the artist counts for so little in the public mind? Has it always been thus? Is there something wrong, perhaps, with the nature of the art work being created in America? Is our system of education lacking in its attitude toward the art product? Should our state and federal governments take a more positive stand toward the cultural development of their citizens?

I realize that I am raising more questions than can possibly be discussed in so brief an address. No doubt the most controversial of these questions is that of the involvement of government in the arts. Central to this issue is the problem as to whether the arts and artists ought to be nurtured in the first place, or whether it is more healthy to let them fend for themselves. One might deduce cogent arguments for both sides of this question. In America nurturing of the arts has traditionally come from private rather than public funds. The kind of free-lance patronage that served the country fairly well in previous times is now becoming more inadequate each year, for reasons that are obvious to all of us. The growing trend toward government involvement is clear, also. Everything points to the eventual admission of the principle at issue, namely, the principle that our government ought actively to concern itself with the welfare of art and professional artists in the United States. Actually the federal government does expend a certain part of its budget for cultural projects, but unfortunately these must always be camouflaged under the heading of education, or of information, or even of national defense—but never as outright support of the arts. That should be changed.

Please don't misconstrue me. I am not asking for a handout for the artists of America. Even on that level the Works Progress Administration proved that artists who were government employees often did valuable work. My belief is that the future will prove that the government needs artists just as badly as artists require government interest. Here is an instance that comes to mind. Our State Department, in a comparatively recent development, has set up more than a hundred fifty cultural centers throughout the world and deposited therein American books, musical scores, phonograph recordings, and paintings as well as educational and scientific materials. (It is a stimulating sight, by the way, to observe one of these cultural centers in action, as I have, in Rome or Tel-Aviv or Rio de Janeiro; to watch a crowded room of young people making contact with intellectual America through its books and music and paintings.) The government purchases the materials necessary for these centers and distributes them abroad. It is only one step further, is it not, to hope to convince the government that since the end product is needed, and worth purchasing, something should be done to stimulate the creation of the product itself, instead of leaving this entirely to the fortuitous chance that some artist will supply what is needed.

I have no doubt that some of you are thinking: "What of the obvious dangers of bureaucratic control of the arts? Is it worth the risk?" Personally, I think it is. The experience of European and Latin American countries in this regard is surely worth something. Subsidies for the arts in those countries are often of an astonishing generosity. These have persisted through periods of economic stress, through wars and violent changes of regime. On more than one occasion I have heard complaints about the dictatorial behavior of a ministry of fine arts, or objections to the academic dud produced by a state-sponsored opera house. But I have never heard anyone in foreign lands hold that the system of state subsidy for the arts should be abandoned because of the dangers it entails. Quite the contrary. They look on us as odd fish for permitting a *laissez-aller* policy in relation to American art. Surely, in a democracy, where each elected government official is a "calculated risk," we ought to be willing to hope for at least as happy a solution as is achieved abroad. Bureaucratic control of the artist in a totalitarian regime is a frightening thing; but in a democracy it should be possible to envisage a liberal encouragement of the arts through allocation of government funds without any permanently dire results.

All this is not unrelated to my main contention that the artist and his work do not count sufficiently in twentieth-century America. People often tend to reflect attitudes of constituted authority. Our people will show more concern for their artists as soon as the government shows more concern for the welfare of art in America. This has been admirably demonstrated in our educational system in regard to the musical training of our youth. In one generation, with a change of attitude on the part of the teachers, the entire picture of music in the schools has altered, so that today we have symphony orchestras and choral ensembles of youngsters that would astonish our European colleagues, if only they knew about them. I cannot honestly report, however, that the young people who

59

sing and play so well have been led to take any but the most conventional attitude to the musical creators whose works they perform. There is a vital link missing here, a link that should enable us to transform a purely perfunctory respect into a living understanding of the idea that surrounds creativity. Somehow, sooner or later, it is that gap in understanding that must be bridged, not only as regards music, but in all the arts. Somehow the reality of the creative man as a person made meaningful for the entire community must be fostered. Creativity in our country depends, in part, on the understanding of all our people. When it is understood as the activity of free and independent men, intent upon the reflection and summation of our own time in beautiful works, art in America will have entered on its most important phase.

Music as an Aspect of the Human Spirit*

I HAVE BEEN ASKED, as part of Columbia University's bicentennial celebration, to improvise on the

* Read as a Radio Address in celebration of Columbia University's two hundredth anniversary in 1954.

theme "Music as an Aspect of the Human Spirit." Most composers would agree, I think, that each new composition constitutes a kind of planned improvisation on a theme. The grander the theme, the more hazardous it is to bring it to fullest fruition. Today's theme is very grand indeed. I very nearly lacked the courage to undertake it, until it struck me that, as a composer, I am occupied each day with this very subject, namely, the expression by way of music of a basic need of the human spirit. To a casual onlooker I may seem to be doing nothing more when I write my scores than the placing of tiny black marks on ruled paper. But, actually, if I now stop to think about it, I am concerned with one of humanity's truly unique achievements: the creation of an art music. In point of fact, I have been concerned with it for more than thirty years, with no lessening of my sense of humility before the majesty of music's expressive power, before its capacity to make manifest a deeply spiritual resource of mankind.

My subject is so immense that it is hard to know where to take hold of it. To begin at the beginning, can we say what music is? Over and over again this question has been asked. The answers given never seem entirely satisfactory for the reason that the boundaries of music are much too extensive and its effects too manifold to be containable within a single definition. Merely to describe its physical impact upon us is none too easy. How, for instance, would I undertake to describe the art of music to a deaf-mute? Even to tell of the effect of a single tone in contradistinction to that of an isolated chord is difficult enough. But how can one adequately encompass the description of an entire symphony? All we know is that for some inscrutable reason most humans vibrate sympathetically to sounds of established pitch when these are coherently organized. These sounds or tones, when produced by instruments or the human voice, singly or in combination, set up sensations that may be deeply moving or merely pleasant or even at times irritating. Whatever the reaction, music that is really attended to rarely leaves the listener indifferent. Musicians react so strongly to musically induced sensations that they become a necessity of daily living.

In saying so much, I have, of course, said very little. One can no more say what music is than one can say what life itself is. But if music is beyond definition, perhaps we can hope to elucidate in what way the art of music is expressive of the human spirit. In a quasi-scientific spirit let me consider, if I may, what I do when I compose. The very idea is a little strange, for one can hardly hope to watch oneself compose. The penalty for so doing is the danger of losing the continuity of one's musical thought. And yet it cannot be claimed that when I compose I am thinking precise thoughts, in the usual meaning of that term. Neither am I mooning over conceptions in the abstract. Instead, I seem to be engrossed in a sphere of essentialized emotions. I stress the word "essentialized," for these emotions are not at all vague. It is important to grasp that fact. They are not vague because they present themselves to the mind of the composer as particularized musical ideas. From the instant of their inception they have specific identity, but it is an identity beyond the power of words to contain or circumscribe. These germinal ideas or essentialized musical thoughts, as I call them, seem to be begging for their own life, asking their creator, the composer, to find the ideal envelope for them, to evolve a shape and color and content that will most fully exploit their creative potential. In this way the profoundest aspirations of man's being are embodied in a pellucid fabric of sonorous materials.

Curious, is it not, that so amorphous and intangible a substance as sound can hold such significance for us? The art of music demonstrates man's ability to transmute the substance of his everyday experience into a body of sound that has coherence and direction and flow, unfolding its own life in a meaningful and natural way in time and in space. Like life itself, music never ends, for it can always be re-created. Thus the greatest moments of the human spirit may be deduced from the greatest moments in music.

It occurs to me to wonder at this point in what way music differs from the other arts in its affirmation of man's spirit. Is it more or less intellectual than literature or the graphic arts? Does it exist merely to melt the human heart, or ought our minds to be engaged primarily in grappling with it? I was interested to read a passage in William James's *Principles of Psychology* that indicated the American philosopher feared excessive indulgence in music

63

would have a debilitating effect on the passive listener. He wasn't entirely serious, I suppose, for he suggests the remedy, "never to suffer one's self to have an emotion at a concert without expressing it afterwards in some active way, such as giving up your seat to a lady in the subway." He exempts from this enervating effect of music those who themselves perform or those who, as he puts it, "are musically gifted enough to take it in a purely intellectual way." Here is an idea that has gained much currency. But do the musically gifted take music in a purely intellectual way? They most certainly do not. They take their music as everyone else does, with this difference: their awareness of the music in its own terms is greater, perhaps, than that of the lay listener, but that is all.

Music is designed, like the other arts, to absorb entirely our mental attention. Its emotional charge is imbedded in a challenging texture, so that one must be ready at an instant's notice to lend attention wherever it is most required in order not to be lost in a sea of notes. The conscious mind follows joyfully in the wake of the composer's invention, playing with the themes as with a ball, extricating the important from the unimportant detail, changing course with each change of harmonic inflection, sensitively reflecting each new color modulation of the subtlest instrumental palette. Music demands an alert mind of intellectual capacity, but it is far from being an intellectual exercise. Musical cerebration as a game for its own sake may fascinate a small minority of experts or specialists, but it has no true significance unless its rhythmic patterns and melodic designs, its harmonic tensions and expressive timbres penetrate the deepest layer of our subconscious mind. It is, in fact, the immediacy of this marriage of mind and heart, this very fusion of musical cerebration directed toward an emotionally purposeful end, that typifies the art of music and makes it different from all other arts.

The power of music is so great and at the same time so direct that people tend to think of it in a static fashion, as if it had always been what we today know it to be. It is scarcely possible to realize how extraordinary the march of Western music has been without considering briefly its historical origins. Musicologists tell us that the music of the early Christian Church was monodic—that is, it was music of a single melodic line. Its finest flower was Gregorian chant. But think what daring it took for composers to attempt the writing of music in more than a single part. This novel conception began to impose itself about a thousand years ago, yet the marvel of it is still a cause for wonder. Our Western music differs from all others mainly in this one aspect: our ability to hear and enjoy a music whose texture is polyphonic, a simultaneous sounding of independent and, at the same time, interdependent contrapuntal melodic lines. It is fascinating to follow the slow growth of musical thinking in the new contrapuntal idiom. Parenthetically, I might add that we of today, because of our great rhythmic and harmonic freedom, are in a better position than our predecessors to appreciate the unconventionalities of these early com-

posers. From the experimental daring of the early con-
trapuntists, whose music had mood and character along
with a certain stiffness and awkwardness, the musical
riches of the Renaissance were born. Musical expressivity
developed in depth and variety, in grace and charm. By
the year 1600 the peak was reached in the sacred and
secular vocal masterpieces of the European continent.
Take note that this was a hundred years before Bach took
up his pen. Out of this many-voiced music, vocal and
instrumental, the science of harmony as we know it
gradually evolved. This was a natural phenomenon resulting from the fact that independent melodic lines, when
sounding together, produced chords.

Then the unexpected happened. These resultant
chords or harmonies, when properly organized, began to
lead a self-sufficient life of their own. The skeletal harmonic progression became more and more significant as a
generating force, until polyphony itself was forced to
share its linear hegemony with the vertical implications of
the underlying harmonies. That giant among composers,
Johann Sebastian Bach, summarized this great moment
in musical history by the perfect wedding of polyphonic
device and harmonic drive. The subsequent forward
sweep of music's development is too well known to
need recounting here. We ought always to remember,
however, that the great age of music did not begin with
Bach and that after him each new age brought its own
particular compositional insight. The Bach summation
hastened the coming of a more limpid and lively style in

the time of Haydn and Mozart. The Viennese masters were followed in turn by the fervent romantics of the nineteenth century, and the past fifty years have brought an anti-romantic reaction and a major broadening of all phases of music's technical resources.

Preoccupation with our own remarkable musical past ought not blind us to the fact that the non-Western world is full of a large variety of musical idioms, most of them in sharp contrast to our own. The exciting rhythms of African drummers, the subtle, melodramatic singing of the Near East, the clangorous ensembles of Indonesia, the incredibly nasal sonority of China and Japan, all these and many others are so different from our own Occidental music as to discourage all hope of a ready understanding. But we realize, nonetheless, that they each in their own way musically mirror cherishable aspects of human consciousness. We needlessly impoverish ourselves in doing so little to make a *rapprochement* between our own art and theirs.

We needlessly impoverish ourselves also in confining so much of our musical interest to a comparatively restricted period of our own music history. An overwhelming amount of the music we normally hear comes from no more than two hundred years of creative composition, principally the eighteenth and nineteenth centuries. No such situation exists in any of the sister arts, nor would it be tolerated. Like the other arts, the art of music has a past, a present, and a future, but, unlike the other arts, the world of music is suffering from a special ailment of its own, namely, a disproportionate interest in its past, and a very limited past at that. Many listeners nowadays appear to be confused. They seem to think that music's future *is* its past. This produces as corollary a painful lack of curiosity as to its present and a reckless disregard for its future.

This question of the public's attitude toward the art of music has become crucial in an age when the general interest in music has expanded beyond the expectations of the most optimistic. Since the advent of radio broadcasting of serious music, the expansion of the recording industry, sophisticated film scores, and television opera and ballet, a true revolution in listening habits is taking place. Serious music is no longer the province of a small elite. No one has yet taken the full measure of this gradual transformation of the past thirty years or calculated its gains and risks for the cause of music. The gains are obvious. The risks come from the fact that millions of listeners are encouraged to consider music solely as a refuge and a consolation from the tensions of everyday living, using the greatest of musical masterpieces as a first line of defense against what are thought to be the inroads of contemporary realism. A pall of conventionalism hangs heavy over today's music horizon. A situation dangerous to music's future is developing in that the natural vigor of present-day musical expression is being jeopardized by this relentless overemphasis on the music of past centuries.

Every composer functions within the limits of his own time and place and in response to the needs of his audience. But for some curious reason, music-lovers persist in believing that music on the highest level ought to be timeless, unaffected by temporal considerations of the here and now. It can easily be shown, however, how far from true that notion is. The music a composer writes makes evident his life experience in a way that is exactly similar to that of any other kind of creative artist, and it is therefore just as closely identified with the aesthetic ideals of the period in which it was created. The composer of today must of necessity take into account the world of today, and his music is very likely to reflect it, even if only negatively. He cannot be expected to execute an about-face for the sole purpose of making contact with an audience that has ears only for music of the past. This dilemma shows no sign of abatement. It isolates more and more the new generation of composers from the public that should be theirs.

How paradoxical the situation is! We live in a time that is acutely aware of the medium of sound. The words "sonic" and "supersonic" are familiar to every schoolboy, and talk of frequencies and decibels is a fairly common usage. Instead of composers being looked to for leadership in such a time, they are relegated to a kind of fringe existence on the periphery of the musical world. It is a fair estimate that seven eighths of the music heard everywhere is music by composers of a past era. Because music needs public performance in order to thrive, the apathetic attitude of the music-loving public to contemporary musical trends has had a depressant effect on present day composers. Under the circumstances one must have tenacity and courage to devote one's life to musical composition.

Despite the absence of stimulus and encouragement, composers in Europe and America have continued to push forward the frontiers of musical exploration. Twentieth-century music has a good record in that respect. It has kept well abreast of the other arts in searching for new expressive resources. The balance sheet would list the following gains: first, a new-found freedom in rhythmic invention. The very modest rhythmic demands of a previous era have been supplanted by the possibilities of a much more challenging rhythmic scheme. The former regularity of an even-measured bar line has given way to a rhythmic propulsion that is more intricate, more vigorous and various, and, certainly, more unpredictable. Most recently certain composers have essayed a music whose basic constructive principle is founded on a strict control of the work's rhythmic factors. Apparently a new species of purely rhythmic logic is envisaged, but with what success it is too soon to know.

Then the area of harmonic possibilities has also been greatly extended in contemporary writing. Leaving behind textbook conventions, harmonic practice has established the premise that any chord may be considered acceptable if it is used appropriately and convincingly. Consonance and dissonance are conceded to be merely relative terms, not absolutes. Principles of tonality have been enlarged almost beyond recognition, while the dodecaphonic method of composing has abandoned them altogether. The young composers of today are the inheritors of a tonal freedom that is somewhat dizzying, but out of this turmoil the new textbooks will be written. Along with harmonic experiment there has been a re-examination of the nature of melody, its range, its intervallic complexity, and its character as binding elements in a composition, especially in respect to thematic relationships. Some few composers have posited the unfamiliar conception of an athematic music, that is, a music whose melodic materials are heard but once and never repeated. All this has come about as part of the larger questioning of the architectonic principles of musical form. This is clearly the end result toward which the newer attitudes are leading. Carried to its logical conclusion, it means an abandonment of long-established constructive principles and a new orientation for music.

Sometimes it seems to me that, in considering the path that music is likely to take in the future, we forget one controlling factor: the nature of the instruments we use. Isn't it possible that we shall wake up one day to find the familiar groups of stringed instruments, brasses, woodwinds, and battery superseded by the invention of an electronic master instrument with unheard-of microtonic divisions of a scale and with totally new sound possibilities, all under the direct control of the composer without benefit of a performing interpreter? Such a machine will emancipate rhythm from the limitations of the performing brain and is likely to make unprecedented demands on the capacity of the human ear. An age that has broken through the sound barrier can hardly be expected to go on producing musical sounds in the time-honored manner of its ancestors. Here, I confess, is a prospect a little frightening to contemplate. For this really may be that music of the future about which Richard Wagner loved to ruminate. All this belongs to the realm of speculation. Only one thing is certain: however arrived at, the process of music and the process of life will always be closely conjoined. So long as the human spirit thrives on this planet, music in some living form will accompany and sustain it and give it expressive meaning.

2. FIVE PERSONALITIES

The Conductor: Serge Koussevitzky*

SERGE KOUSSEVITZKY has now completed his first twenty years as leader of the Boston Symphony Orchestra. Year after year during those two decades he has consistently carried through a policy of performing orchestral works, old and new, by American composers. In so doing he has not been alone. Other conductors and other orchestras have introduced numerous works by Americans during the same period. But just because he was not alone in nurturing the growth of an American music, it is all the more remarkable that we think of his sponsorship of the native composer as something unique —something unprecedented and irreplaceable.

It is easy to foresee that the story of Serge Kousse-

* This article, written in 1944 during Serge Koussevitzky's lifetime, was published in the *Musical Quarterly*. In order to retain the sense of contemporaneity, nothing has been changed.

vitzky and the American composer will someday take on the character of a legend. Here at least is one legend that will have been well founded. Since circumstances placed me among the earliest of the conductor's American "protégés," I should like to put down an eye witness account, so to speak, of how the legend grew—what it is based on, how it functions, and what it means in our present-day musical culture.

I first met the future conductor of the Boston Symphony at his apartment in Paris in the spring of 1923, shortly after the announcement of his appointment had been made. My teacher, Nadia Boulanger, brought me to see him. It was the period of the Concerts Koussevitzky, given at the Paris Opéra each spring and fall. It was typical that at the Concerts Koussevitzky all the new and exciting European novelties were introduced. Mademoiselle Boulanger, knowing the Russian conductor's interest in new creative talents of all countries, took it for granted that he would want to meet a young composer from the country he was about to visit for the first time. That she was entirely correct in her assumption was immediately evident from the interest he showed in the orchestral score under my arm. It was a *Cortège Macabre*, an excerpt from a ballet I had been working on under the guidance of Mademoiselle Boulanger. With all the assurance of youth—I was twenty-two years old at the time—I played it for him. Without hesitation he promised to perform the piece during his first season in Boston.

That visit must have been one of the first of many

meetings that Dr. Koussevitzky has had with American composers. The submitting of a new work to Dr. Koussevitzky is always something of an ordeal for a composer. He is well known for being outspoken in his reaction to new music. If he likes a composition he generally likes it wholeheartedly, and the composer leaves his presence walking on thin air. (After all, it means a performance by the Boston Symphony Orchestra!) If he doesn't like it, it means that other conductors may perform it, but the special atmosphere that surrounds a Koussevitzky première will be lacking. That sense of "specialness" is part of the legend—it has seeped through even to composers who have never had occasion to show their works to the Russian director. But they all dream of that occasion; just as every ten-year-old American boy dreams of being President someday, so every twenty-year-old American composer dreams of being played by Koussevitzky.

It is not simply a matter of the quality of the performance, fine as that is likely to be, that accounts for the prestige attached to a performance by the Boston Symphony under its present leader. It is rather the "philosophy" behind the playing of the work that, in the final analysis, makes the difference. It is the nature of that "philosophy" that gives to the relationship of Dr. Koussevitzky and the American composer its more than local interest and significance.

Consider, for a moment, what was normal procedure for the introduction of native works into the symphonic repertoire during the first years of the twenties. Most char-

acteristic of the period, as I remember it, was an unholy
concentration on first performances. A new work seemed
automatically to lose whatever attraction it may have had
after a first hearing. Even when a composition was well
received locally, its repetition by other orchestras was by
no means guaranteed. But worse than this seasonal dab-
bling in novelties was the patent lack of conviction on the
part of conductors (with certain exceptions, of course) as
to the value of the new pieces they were presenting. That
lack of conviction was reflected, more often than not, in
the attitude of the men in the orchestra. In an atmosphere
of distrust and indifference works were likely to be under-
rehearsed and played without conviction. After all, if the
music really wasn't worth much, why waste time rehears-
ing it? And in the end the audience, sensing the lack of
any sustained policy on the part of the conductor or symphonic organization, concluded quite justly that the playing of any new American work might be regarded as a
bore, to be quietly suffered for the sake of some misguided chauvinism on the part of the management.

In Boston, under the Koussevitzky regime, all these
things were ordered differently. Taking its keynote from
the attitude of the conductor himself, a musical New Deal
was instituted for the American composer. Fundamentally
this New Deal was founded upon the solid rock of Dr.
Koussevitzky's unwavering belief in the musical creative
force of our time. He had always had that faith—in
Russia it had been Scriabine, Stravinsky, and Prokofieff
who aroused his enthusiasm; in Paris it was Ravel and

Honegger (among others). He had simply transplanted to our own country his basic confidence in the creative powers of our world.

That confidence is unshakable—it is an essential part of the man. Someplace deep down Dr. Koussevitzky is himself a composer—not because of the few works he has actually written, but because he has a profound understanding for what it means to be a composer. I have never met a man who loved music more passionately than Serge Koussevitzky. But when he thinks of music he doesn't conjure up a pristine and abstract art—he thinks rather of a living, organic matter brought into being by men who are thoroughly alive. He loves music, yes—but never for an instant does he forget the men who create music. That is why it is no mere conventional phrase when he says: "We in America must have confidence in our own composers." Essentially that confidence is born out of a love for the historic role played by composers of all ages in building up the art of music as we know it. I can personally attest to the fact that he meant every word of it literally when he recently wrote: "I feel a rage and my whole body begins to tremble in a protest against conservatism and lack of understanding that it is the composer who gives us the greatest joy we have in the art of music."

It should be clear by now that every instinct in the man cries out against the current notion that present-day creative activity is empty and sterile. All history has convinced him that the creative force in music is a continuous one, and that each generation adds its mite to the sum

77

total of musical culture. Dr. Koussevitzky would be the first to allow that certain ages have been more fortunate in their composers than others. But if there has ever been a completely impotent age, as far as musical creativity goes, he has never heard of it.

He has explained his point of view at some length in a recent interview:

"Every great, or less great, or even little, composer brings something to the art of music which makes the art great in its entirety. Each one brings his portion. In examination of his music we can see how real a composer is. We can see whether his technique is perfect; whether he knows how the orchestra and the individual instruments sound and whether or not he has something to say, no matter what the degree of importance. Sometimes a single man has one single word to say in all his life and that one word may be as important as the lifework of a great genius. We need that word . . . and so does the genius himself need that word."

What vitality and energy he has expended on the uncovering of "that word"! For no one must imagine that his over-all sympathy for the practicing composer produces a hit-or-miss method of choosing compositions for his programs. On the contrary, few conductors have been as finicky in their choice of works. If it were merely a matter of statistics, other conductors have outdistanced him in the percentage of new works played. Absolutely nothing but Dr. Koussevitzky's private conviction as to the value of a work will result in its performance. But once his mind is made up, it doesn't matter whether the chosen work is long, abstruse, dissonant, difficult to perform, difficult to comprehend—that work will be heard.

No composer who has lived through a week of rehearsals at Symphony Hall in preparation for an important première can possibly forget the experience. The program for the week is carefully planned so that the major portion of the rehearsal period may be devoted to the new work. To Dr. Koussevitzky each untried composition is a fresh adventure—the outcome is as unpredictable as the delivery of an unborn babe. The composer is present, of course, for morning rehearsals; these are generally followed by evening discussions with the conductor in preparation for the next day's work. Throughout the week conductor and composer may run the gamut of emotions from liveliest elation to darkest misgivings. But come what may, by Friday afternoon the work is ready for its public test. The conductor walks to the podium with a full sense of his responsibility to the composer and to the work. No wonder other premières seem perfunctory by comparison!

Out of his sense of responsibility to the creative talent of our time comes his belief in his role as educator. He has often told me that the director of an orchestra should be the musical leader of his community. It is not enough that he himself have faith in the work he plays; the orchestra and the public he serves must also be convinced of its value. Thomas Mann might have had Serge Koussevitzky in mind when he wrote: "Great conductors of music are educators, for that is their *métier*. And if they are more than just professional experts—which they have to be to be great—their will to educate, their belief in education reach into ethics and enter the political-human sphere."

From an educational standpoint winning over the orchestra has been a comparatively easy task. No other group of professional men that I know has so open-minded and wide-awake an attitude toward new music. Thinking back twenty years, I would say that that has not always been the case. But apparently Dr. Koussevitzky has forgotten the early days, for he recently stated: "I've never had the slightest difficulty with the orchestra men concerning our programs. The musicians were and are always co-operative and interested, no matter how difficult a work may be to play. In fact, the harder a work is, the more willingly they devote themselves to it."

The public and the critics have naturally proved a more recalcitrant factor. There may still be some subscribers who turn in their tickets to the box office at the threat of a new work on the program. But by and large Dr. Koussevitzky has long since established the principle with the majority of his listeners that a well-balanced symphonic diet must include Vitamin C: contemporary music. For years they have swallowed it bravely; by now they are one of the healthiest audiences we have.

As for the critics, it seems to me that Dr. Koussevitzky has adopted an entirely realistic view. He does not attempt to underestimate their power to influence, temporarily, the reading public's reaction for or against a young composer whose reputation is still in the making. On the other hand, when they write encomiums it simply makes his own pioneering easier. But courage in the face of opposition is second nature to him. Many a time he has chosen to repeat a work on the heels of adverse newspaper comment. More than once, as consistent champion of some contemporary composer, he has had the keen satisfaction of watching the public and the critics gradually accept his view.

Unlike certain of his colleagues, Dr. Koussevitzky does not lose all interest in the American composer once he has stepped out of the concert hall. Composers are his daily preoccupation. In recent years he has devoted more and more time to a consideration of their economic setup. He has been profoundly disturbed at the realization that the great majority of our composers devote the major part of their time, not to writing music, but to the gaining of a livelihood. He can never accustom himself to the thought that in this rich country of ours no plan exists that would provide composers with a modicum of financial security for the production of serious works of music. His active mind has been busily at work. Who but Dr. Koussevitzky could have written: "A far reaching and wise plan must be worked out to establish a permanent composers' fund which will cover the essential and immediate needs of the living American composer"?

It is typical that he has not been content passively to await the setting up of a Composers' Fund. As an immediate gesture, he established the Koussevitzky Music

Foundation in memory of his wife, Natalie Koussevitzky, who, during her lifetime, had loyally seconded his every move in behalf of the living composer. Although the Foundation has been in existence for only a few years, it has already commissioned more than a dozen composers to write new orchestral and chamber-music works. This carries on Dr. Koussevitzky's self-imposed task, instituted many years ago in Russia and continued in France—namely, the stimulation of the creative energies of composers of every nationality through publication, performance, and the special ordering of compositions. It is moving, to say the least, to contemplate this world-famous conductor, on the threshold of seventy, expending his time and energy so that more and more music may be brought into the world.

Can it be pure chance that the twenty years of Dr. Koussevitzky's leadership—1924 to 1944—have coincided with the period during which American symphonic literature has come of age? During that time he has given a first hearing to sixty-six American compositions. Despite that record I once heard him make the statement that American composition would only really come into its own when it was given under the baton of American-born conductors. What a remark to come from a conductor famous for his eloquent performances of American works! What a disinterested, astute, and prophetic remark! And how fortunate we shall be if our native-born conductors, inspired by the example of their great Russian-American confrere, will know how to comprehend and carry forward the invaluable contribution he has made to the flowering of a true American musical culture.

The Teacher: Nadia Boulanger

IT IS ALMOST FORTY YEARS since first I rang the bell at Nadia Boulanger's Paris apartment and asked her to accept me as her composition pupil. Any young musician may do the same thing today, for Mademoiselle Boulanger lives at the same address in the same apartment and teaches with the same formidable energy. The only difference is that she was then comparatively little known outside the Paris music world and today there are few musicians anywhere who would not concede her to be the most famous of living composition teachers.

Our initial meeting had taken place in the Palace of Fontainebleau several months before that first Paris visit. Through the initiative of Walter Damrosch a summer music school for American students was established in a wing of the palace in 1921 and Nadia Boulanger was on the staff as teacher of harmony. I arrived, fresh out of

Brooklyn, aged twenty, and all agog at the prospect of studying composition in the country that had produced Debussy and Ravel. A fellow-student told me about Mademoiselle Boulanger and convinced me that a look-in on her harmony class would be worth my while. I needed convincing—after all, I had already completed my harmonic studies in New York and couldn't see how a harmony teacher could be of any help to me. What I had not foreseen was the power of Mademoiselle Boulanger's personality and the special glow that informs her every discussion of music whether on the simplest or the most exalted plane.

The teaching of harmony is one thing; the teaching of advanced composition is something else again. The reason they differ so much is that harmonic procedures are deduced from known common practice while free composition implies a subtle mixing of knowledge and instinct for the purpose of guiding the young composer toward a goal that can only be dimly perceived by both student and teacher. Béla Bartók used to claim that teaching composition was impossible to do well; he himself would have no truck with it. Mademoiselle Boulanger would undoubtedly agree that it is difficult to do well—and then go right on trying.

Actually Nadia Boulanger was quite aware that as a composition teacher she labored under two further disadvantages: she was not herself a regularly practicing composer and in so far as she composed at all she must of necessity be listed in that unenviable category of the woman composer. Everyone knows that the high achievement of women musicians as vocalists and instrumentalists has no counterpart in the field of musical composition. This historically poor showing has puzzled more than one observer. It is even more inexplicable when one considers the reputation of women novelists and poets, of painters and designers. Is it possible that there is a mysterious element in the nature of musical creativity that runs counter to the nature of the feminine mind? And yet there are more women composers than ever writing today, writing, moreover, music worth playing. The future may very well have a different tale to tell; for the present, however, no woman's name will be found on the list of world-famous composers.

To what extent Mademoiselle Boulanger had serious ambitions as composer has never been entirely established. She has published a few short pieces, and once told me that she had aided the pianist and composer Raoul Pugno in the orchestration of an opera of his. Mainly she was credited with the training of her gifted younger sister Lili, whose composing talent gained her the first Prix de Rome ever accorded a woman composer in more than a century of prize giving. It was an agonizing blow when Lili fell seriously ill and died in 1918 at the age of twenty-four. It was then that Nadia established the pattern of life that I found her living with her Russian-born mother in the Paris of the twenties.

Curiously enough I have no memory of discussing the role of women in music with Mademoiselle. What-

ever her attitude may have been, she herself was clearly a
phenomenon for which there was no precedent. In my
own mind she was a continuing link in that long tradition
of the French intellectual woman in whose salon philosophy was expounded and political history made. In similar
fashion Nadia Boulanger had her own salon where musical aesthetics was argued and the muscial future engen-
dered. It was there that I saw, and sometimes even met,
the musical great of Paris: Maurice Ravel, Igor Stravinsky,
Albert Roussel, Darius Milhaud, Arthur Honegger,
Francis Poulenc, Georges Auric. She was the friend of
Paul Valéry and Paul Claudel, and liked to discuss the
latest works of Thomas Mann, of Proust, and André
Gide. Her intellectual interests and wide acquaintance-
ship among artists in all fields were an important stimulus
to her American students: through these interests she
whetted and broadened their cultural appetites.

It would be easy to sketch a portrait of Mademoiselle
Boulanger as a personality in her own right. Those who
meet her or hear her talk are unlikely to forget her physical presence. Of medium height and pleasant features,
she gave off, even as a young woman, a kind of objective
warmth. She had none of the ascetic intensity of a Martha
Graham or the toughness of a Gertrude Stein. On the
contrary, in those early days she possessed an almost old-
fashioned womanliness—a womanliness that seemed quite
unaware of it own charm. Her low-heeled shoes and
long black skirts and pince-nez glasses contrasted strangely
with her bright intelligence and lively temperament. In

more recent years she has become smaller and thinner, quasi nun-like in appearance. But her low-pitched voice is as resonant as ever and her manner has lost none of its decisiveness.

My purpose here, however, is to concentrate on her principal attribute, her gift as teacher. As her reputation spread, students came to her not only from America but also from Turkey, Poland, Chile, Japan, England, Norway, and many other countries. How, I wonder, would each one of them describe what Mademoiselle gave him as teacher? How indeed does anyone describe adequately what is learned from a powerful teacher? I myself have never read a convincing account of the progress from student stage to that of creative maturity through a teacher's ministrations. And yet it happens: some kind of magic does indubitably rub off on the pupil. It begins, perhaps, with the conviction that one is in the presence of an exceptional musical mentality. By a process of osmosis one soaks up attitudes, principles, reflections, knowledge. That last is a key word: it is literally exhilarating to be with a teacher for whom the art one loves has no secrets.

Nadia Boulanger knew everything there was to know about music; she knew the oldest and the latest music, pre-Bach and post-Stravinsky, and knew it cold. All technical know-how was at her fingertips: harmonic transposition, the figured bass, score reading, organ registration, instrumental techniques, structural analyses, the school fugue and the free fugue, the Greek modes and Gregorian chant. Needless to say this list is far from exhaustive. She was particularly intrigued by new musical developments. I can still remember the eagerness of her curiosity concerning my jazz-derived rhythms of the early twenties, a corner of music that had somehow escaped her. Before long we were exploring polyrhythmic devices together—their cross-pulsations, their notation, and especially their difficulty of execution intrigued her. This was typical, nothing under the heading of music could possibly be thought of as foreign. I am not saying that she liked or even approved of all kinds of musical expression —far from it. But she had the teacher's consuming need to know how all music functions, and it was that kind of inquiring attitude that registered on the minds of her students.

More important to the budding composer than Mademoiselle Boulanger's technical knowledge was her way of surrounding him with an air of confidence. (The reverse—her disapproval, I am told, was annihilating in its effect.) In my own case she was able to extract from a composer of two-page songs and three-page piano pieces a full-sized ballet lasting thirty-five minutes. True, no one has ever offered to perform the completed ballet, but the composing of it proved her point—I was capable of more than I myself thought possible. This mark of confidence was again demonstrated when, at the end of my three years of study, Mademoiselle Boulanger asked me to write an organ concerto for her first American tour, knowing full well that I had only a nodding acquaintance with the king of instruments and that I had never heard a note of my own orchestration. "Do you really think I can do it?" I asked hopefully. "*Mais oui*" was the firm reply—and so I did.

Mademoiselle gave the world première of the work— a Symphony for organ and orchestra—on January 11, 1925, under the baton of Walter Damrosch. My parents, beaming, sat with me in a box. Imagine our surprise when the conductor, just before beginning the next work on the program, turned to his audience and said: "If a young man, at the age of twenty-three, can write a symphony like that, in five years he will be ready to commit murder!" The asperities of my harmonies had been too much for the conductor, who felt that his faithful subscribers needed reassurance that he was on their side. Mademoiselle Boulanger, however, was not to be swayed; despite her affection for Mr. Damrosch she wavered not in the slightest degree in her favorable estimate of my symphony.

All musicians, like the lay music-lover, must in the end fall back upon their own sensibilities for value judgments. I am convinced that it is Mademoiselle Boulanger's perceptivity as musician that is at the core of her teaching. She is able to grasp the still-uncertain contours of an incomplete sketch, examine it, and foretell the probable and possible ways in which it may be developed. She is expert in picking flaws in any work in progress, and knowing why they are flaws. At the period when I was her pupil she had but one all-embracing principle, namely, the desirability of aiming first and fore-

most at the creation of what she called *"la grande ligne"*—
the long line in music. Much was included in that
phrase: the sense of forward motion, of flow and continuity in the musical discourse; the feeling for inevitability, for the creating of an entire piece that could be
thought of as a functioning entity. These generalizations
were given practical application: her eye, for instance, was
always trained upon the movement of the bass line as
controlling agent for the skeletal frame of the harmony's
progressive action. Her sense of contrast was acute; she
was quick to detect *longueurs* and any lack of balance.
Her teaching, I suppose, was French in that she always
stressed clarity of conception and elegance in proportion.
It was her broadness of sympathy that made it possible
for her to apply these general principles to the music of
young men and women of so many different nationalities.

Many of these observations are based, of course, on
experiences of a good many years ago. Much has happened to music since that time. The last decade, in particular, cannot have been an easy time for the teacher of
composition, and especially for any teacher of the older
generation. The youngest composers have taken to wor-
shiping at strange shrines. Their attempt to find new
constructive principles through the serialization of the
chromatic scale has taken music in a direction for which
Mademoiselle showed little sympathy in former years.
The abandonment of tonality and the adoption of We-
bernian twelve-tone methods by many of the younger
Frenchmen and even by Igor Stravinsky in his later years

cannot have been a cause for rejoicing on the Rue Ballu. And yet, I have heard Mademoiselle Boulanger speak warmly of the music of the leader of the new movement, Pierre Boulez. Knowing the musician she is, I feel certain that she will find it possible to absorb the best of the newer ideas into her present-day thinking.

In the meantime it must be a cause for profound satisfaction to Mademoiselle Boulanger that she has guided the musical destiny of so many gifted musicians: Igor Markevitch, Jean Françaix, and Marcelle de Manziarly in France; Americans like Walter Piston, Virgil Thomson, Roy Harris, Marc Blitzstein, among the older men, Elliott Carter, David Diamond, Irving Fine, Harold Shapero, Arthur Berger among the middle generation, and youngsters like Easley Blackwood during the fifties.

In 1959, when Harvard University conferred an honorary degree on Nadia Boulanger, a modest gesture was made toward recognition of her standing as teacher and musician. America, unfortunately, has no reward commensurate with what Nadia Boulanger has contributed to our musical development. But, in the end, the only reward she would want is the one she already has: the deep affection of her many pupils everywhere.

The Composer: Igor Stravinsky

HIS PERSONALITY:

For a long time I have wondered about the exact nature of the personality of Stravinsky. Everyone agrees that Stravinsky possesses one of the most individual natures of our time. But to get at the essence of it is another matter.

Certain great composers are literally drenched in their own personal atmosphere. One thinks immediately of Chopin, or the later Beethoven, or the mature Wagner. On the other hand, if you don't listen closely, there are times when you might mistake Mozart for Haydn, or Bach for Handel, or even Ravel for Debussy. I cannot ever remember being fooled by the music of Stravinsky. It invariably sounds like music that only he could have written.

Why? I'm sure I don't know . . . but I keep wondering about it. Musicians will tell you that you must take the music apart, see how it is made, then put it together again, and you will have the answer. I've tried it, but it doesn't really work. Knowing Stravinsky the man helps a little, but not enough. At home he is a charming host, a man with clearly defined ideas and a sharp tongue . . . but the music seems to exist on a suprapersonal plane, in an aural world of its own.

It is his work of the last few years that holds the mystery tightest. One thinks of the *Mass*, the *Canticum Sacrum*, or of *Threni* . . . these works, in some curious way, seem strangely removed from everyday "events," and yet they remain for the most part profoundly human. Sobriety is the keynote—it seems hardly possible to create a music of less sensuous appeal. Nevertheless there are moments of an enriched texture—all the more rare and precious because they seem measured out so carefully. In these works thought and instinct are inextricably wedded, as they should be.

Perhaps it is just because the secret cannot be extracted that the fascination of Stravinsky's personality continues to hold us.

HIS WORKMANSHIP:

A close examination of the Russian master's textural fabric, especially his harmonic textures, makes it clear that we are dealing with a mind that doesn't hear "straight," in the usual sense. It is the rightness of his "wrong" so-

93

lutions that fascinates one. Marcel Proust must have had
something of the same notion in mind when, in considering Flaubert's prose style, he talked about "great writers
who do not know how to write." One might say that
Stravinsky doesn't know how to compose in the sense of
Hindemith or Milhaud. He lacks their facility or virtuosity, a kind of facility and virtuosity that allows the
notes to run to their predetermined places—almost, one
might say, without more than an assist from their composers. With Stravinsky one senses that the place of each
note in each melody and chord has been found for it only
after a process of meticulous elimination, and the place
found is usually so unexpected and original that one can
imagine the notes themselves being surprised at finding
themselves situated where they are—"out of place," so to
speak. Facility, in Stravinsky's case, would have been
ruinous. And yet, by virtue of living long enough, and
adding a work year by year to his output, he has in the
end amassed a considerable *oeuvre*.

HIS INFLUENCE:

If we can gauge the vitality of a composer's work by
the extent of his influence, then Stravinsky's record is an
enviable one. For almost half a century his music has ex-
ercised a continuing hold that is without parallel since
Wagner's day. In the twentieth century only Debussy cast
a comparable spell, and that was of a limited nature and

of a single style. It is one of the curiosities of contemporary musical history that Stravinsky has been able to influence two succeeding generations in ways diametrically opposed.

Because of Stravinsky the period 1917–27 was the decade of the displaced accent and the polytonal chord. Few escaped the impact of his personality. The frenetic dynamism and harmonic daring of *Le Sacre* were reflected in other ballets, Prokofieff's *Age of Steel*, Chávez's *H.P.* (Horse Power), Carpenter's *Skyscrapers*. Antheil's *Ballet Mécanique* was a *reductio ad absurdum* of Stravinsky's emphasis on furious rhythms and pitiless dissonances.

Then suddenly, with almost no warning, Stravinsky executed an about-face that startled and confused everyone. Everyone but the composers, that is. For despite repeated critical accusations of sterility and an apathetic public response, many composers rallied to the new cause of neoclassicism. Once more Stravinsky had called the tune.

In America one can trace a straight line from Roger Sessions' *Symphony No. 1* (1927) to Harold Shapero's *Symphony for Classical Orchestra* (1947). Among the generation of the mid-forties it was easy to identify a Stravinsky school: Shapero, Haieff, Berger, Lessard, Smit, Foss, Fine.

Looking ahead, one can foresee still a third type of Stravinsky influence, based upon his recent commerce with Central European serialism. Nothing in Stravinsky's past had suggested the possibility of his becoming immersed in the seminal scores of Anton Webern. Here we have the most surprising twist of all. How long this interest will last no one can say. But one result is predictable: there are certain to be younger composers who will plot their own lines in accordance with Stravinsky's latest absorptions.

Isn't it surprising that, in his eighth decade, Stravinsky is still writing problem music? All the other composers over fifty—the famous ones, I mean—are turning out more or less what is expected of them. It seems a long time since we got a jolt from Hindemith. Schönberg's last works were problematical certainly, but in the same way they had been for the preceding thirty years. Milhaud, Britten, Piston are all sticking close to form. Only Stravinsky manages to mix his elements, including even the familiar ones, in such a way that no one can predict just where he will be taking us next.

But perhaps the most impressive point of all is that over and beyond the question of influence there remains in Stravinsky's music an irreducible core that defies imitation. The essence of the man—his special "tone," his very personal brand of seriousness, the non-academic texture of his music—in short, the sum total of his extraordinary individuality, has never to my knowledge been adequately described, let alone imitated. Despite the widespread influence of his music Stravinsky as a composer remains a singularly remote and removed figure, a composer whose passport to the future needs no signature other than his own.

The Critic: Paul Rosenfeld

IT ISN'T OFTEN that a composer wants to talk to people about a man who wrote music criticism. Critics and composers are usually considered, by definition, to be incompatible. But Paul Rosenfeld was someone special. Except for the start of his career he never had a job on a daily newspaper. Most of his writing about music appeared in books and magazines and was read during his lifetime by a restricted audience. He never wrote in a journalistic style. His prose was richly expressive, sometimes perhaps too richly expressive, with an occasional paragraph in a jargon all his own. But the thing that made him special was not so much what he said or how he said it, but the very attitude he took toward the whole art of music.

To me the exciting thing about Rosenfeld's criticism is the fact that for once a critic completely involved himself in the very music he was criticizing. I'd like to explain that conception of "the involvement of the critic," as I call it. People often talk as if they imagine it is the duty of the critic to remain severely aloof in order to guarantee a balanced judgment. But that is not my idea. A critic, it must be said, is not just a detached bystander whose job may be considered finished when he has given the composer a casual hearing. No, a critic is just as much a member of our musical civilization as any composer is. He ought to be just as deeply involved, just as completely responsible, just as serious when he writes his criticism as a composer is when he writes his music.

Paul Rosenfeld understood all that. Whether he judged a work good or bad, he judged it as a part of himself, not something outside himself—not something he could take or leave—but something of immense significance to him, and therefore of significance to America, and through America to the world. It is always surprising to find how little our critics seem to want to involve themselves in that sense. They exist on the outer fringe of music—looking on from the outside at what is being done, but seldom taking a really active part in it. If all this is true, then they are a shortsighted lot, for whether they like it or not, we are all in the same musical boat.

Rosenfeld demonstrated his own involvement most clearly in his approach to contemporary music. I very well remember the excitement of reading his first articles about the young Stravinsky and the young Ernest Bloch. That must have been around 1919 or 1920. Later I first saw mention of the name of Roger Sessions in a Rosenfeld article in the *Dial* magazine. It is easy enough to appreciate who these men are now. But in those days their music was being vilified in the daily press by writers whose names today are best forgotten.

The American scene in particular was a consuming interest of Rosenfeld. He believed passionately in the emergence of an important school of contemporary American composers. He was one of the very first to affirm the talents of men like Roy Harris and the Mexican Carlos Chávez. As for myself, I owe him a special debt. He not only went far out on a limb in relation to my music in its earliest stages but also saw to it that I had a patron to help me through those first difficult years. He didn't think the critic's role was done when he had written a good notice on a new composition. He was concerned about what the next work of the composer would be, and the one after that, and how the composer was going to live while writing these next works.

The unknown and unheralded composer remained an absorbing concern of Rosenfeld through all his writing years. Not everyone he championed has received public recognition. But that was part of the game as he saw it. He wasn't interested in always playing safe with his music judgments. He took chances when some years back he wrote enthusiastically about the neglected Charles Ives or the fifteen-year-old Lukas Foss. He took chances when he gave a preeminent place to the music of Leo Ornstein or Edgard Varèse. He took chances when he endorsed the music of the little-known American composer Charles Mills.

It is not the exactitude of his judgments that is impressive so much as the sharpness of his sensitivity to music. He felt himself at home in an amazing number of different styles and personalities. It was music as a whole that fascinated him rather than any one phase of it. His reactions to the music of masters like Bach or Palestrina were no less keen and perceptive than his reactions to modern music.

In a sense Paul Rosenfeld was, I suppose, first a music-lover, and second a music critic. If so, I wish there were more such music-lovers among our music critics.

The Pianist: William Kapell*

DEAR ANNA LOU: When a dear friend is lost to us we try to bring some solace to the nearest of kin by writing a letter. Many thousands of music-lovers in many parts of the world must have felt that impulse when they learned of your husband's tragic end on October 29. I too had that impulse, and writing you this letter my hope is

* William Kapell died in an airplane accident in 1953.

that I may possibly express some of the things that are
certainly in the hearts of William Kapell's many admirers.

When I think of Willie I think of him as having been
above all else the personification of the artist. Except for
yourself and the children, I never recall discussing anything but music with him. The singleness of his passion
for the art we both loved was almost frightening, even to
a composer like myself. It was as if the sound of music
created a hypnotic spell about him—and whether it was
sound made by himself or sound listened to made little
essential difference. When music was heard nothing else
mattered. I know that this is said to be true for most
musicians, but for the most part that is a pleasant fiction;
in Willie's case it was quite literally true. As you well
know, to him a house without a piano was no better than
an empty shell; to find himself in a situation where no
piano was within easy reach was physically intolerable. In
that connection he more than once reminded me of
George Gershwin—seeing either of them in a room where
there was a piano meant that sooner or later the man and
the instrument would meet.

All this has little significance compared with the way
in which William was profoundly the artist, both in his
very nature and in the symbolic role he was fated to play
in the concert world. The artist in him was startlingly
evident in his person and in his performing gift: he was
passionate, intense, restless, devoted, in love with perfection as a goal, forever striving toward that goal—straining
toward it, even. At times his friends must have seemed

inadequate and distant to him, for the force and drive of his temperament were such as necessarily to make him dissatisfied when confronted with the signs of sweet reasonableness. His questioning and demanding spirit gave off sparks of a youthfulness that never left him. Willie, if he had lived, would always have remained a youthful artist, in the best sense of that term. The search for artistic growth, the ideal of maturity was a central and continuing preoccupation with him. Emerson once wrote that the artist is "pitiful." He meant, I suppose, that the true artist can never be entirely satisfied with the work he does. William Kapell was that kind of true artist.

And yet he was among the few top pianists of our time. Why? What qualities were particularly his? There were brilliance and drama in his playing, songfulness and excitement. On the platform he had the fire and abandon that alone can arouse audiences to fever pitch. He knew his power, and I have no doubt was sometimes frightened by it. The big public can be a potential menace, after all; it can elicit the best and the worst from the artist. Characteristically, when playing on the stage, Willie often turned his head away from the auditorium, the better to forget us, I imagine. Nevertheless, even when most lost within himself, he instinctively projected his playing into the hall, for he was indubitably the performer. I cannot conceive of his ever having given a dull performance—an erratic one perhaps, a misguided or stylistically incongruous one maybe, but invariably one that was electric and alive.

We both know that he was, at times, an easy target for the reviewers of the daily press. He exaggerated their importance, ignored the good things said, and remembered only the bad. I always took this to be a measure of his own seriousness. The successful performer of today cannot plead ignorance of his own playing. He has the recorded disc for mirror. Willie knew better than anyone when he was in top form; to be unjustly evaluated after such performances pained and tortured him. Unlike the composer in a similar position, he could not expect justification from posterity. No wonder he was unusually nervous before stepping on the platform. Like every basically romantic artist, he never could predict what was about to happen on the stage, but on the other hand the satisfaction of an outstanding performance must have been enormous.

I shall always treasure the thought of William's deep attachment to my own music. He never tired of telling me what my music meant to him, and I, on my part, never ceased being surprised at the intensity of his feeling for it. What was most surprising was his fondness for the most forbidding aspects of my music; he repeatedly played precisely those pieces that his audiences were least likely to fathom. He played them with a verve and grandeur and authority that only a front-rank pianist is able to bring to unfamiliar music. He played them, I often felt, in a spirit of defiance: defiance of managers with their cautious notions of what was right and fitting for a Kapell program; defiance of the audience that had come to hear him in works from the regular repertoire; played them, one might almost say, in defiance of his own best interests. In actuality I believe he played them in order to satisfy a deep need—the need every artist has to make connection with the music of his own time. I am touched and moved at the thought of the high regard in which he held them. His programming of new music was an act of faith; it was Willie's contribution toward a solution of one of the most disturbing factors in our musical life: namely, the loss of connection between the performer and the contemporary composer of his own time.

When William died he was expecting a new piano work from my pen. It was a promise I had gladly given him. It is a promise I intend to keep, and when the work is written I can only hope that it will be worthy of the best in William Kapell.

My love and sympathy are with you.

At the Thought of Mozart

PAUL VALERY ONCE WROTE: "The definition of beauty is easy: it is that which makes us despair." On reading that phrase I immediately thought of Mozart. Admittedly despair is an unusual word to couple with the Viennese master's music. And yet, isn't it true that any incommensurable thing sets up within us a kind of despair? There is no way to *seize* the Mozart music. This is true even for a fellow-composer, any composer, who, being a composer, rightfully feels a special sense of kinship, even a happy familiarity, with the hero of Salzburg. After all, we can pore over him, dissect him, marvel or carp at him. But in the end there remains something that will not be *seized*. That is why, each time a Mozart work begins—I am thinking of the finest examples now—we composers listen with a certain awe and wonder, not unmixed with despair. The wonder we share with everyone;

the despair comes from the realization that only this one man at this one moment in musical history could have created works that seem so effortless and so close to perfection. The possession of any rare beauty, any perfect love, sets up a similar distress, no doubt.

Mozart had one inestimable advantage as compared with the composers of later times: he worked within the "perfection of a common language." Without such a common language the Mozartean approach to composition and the triumphs that resulted would have been impossible. Matthew Arnold once put it this way: during such a time "you can descend into yourself and produce the best of your thought and feeling naturally, and without an overwhelming and in some degree morbid effort; for then all the people around you are more or less doing the same thing." It has been a long time since composers of the Western world have been so lucky.

Because of that I detect a certain envy mixed with their affectionate regard for Mozart as man and musician. Composers, normally, tend to be sharply critical of the works of their colleagues, ancient or modern. Mozart himself exemplified this rule. But it doesn't hold true for other composers and Mozart. A kind of love affair has been going on between them ever since the eight-year-old prodigy made the acquaintance of Johann Christian Bach in London. It cooled off somewhat in the romantic nineteenth century, only to be renewed with increased ardor in our own time. It is a strange fact that in the twentieth century it has been the more complex composers who have admired him most—perhaps because they needed him most. Busoni said that Mozart was "the most perfect example of musical talent we have ever had." Richard Strauss, after composing *Salome* and *Elektra*, paid him the ultimate compliment of abandoning his own style in order to refashion himself on a Mozartean model. Schönberg called himself a "pupil of Mozart," knowing full well that such a statement from the father of atonality would astonish. Darius Milhaud, Ernst Toch, and a host of composer-teachers quote him again and again as favored example for their students. Paradoxically, it appears that precisely those composers who left music more complicated than they found it are proudest to be counted among the Mozart disciples.

I number myself among the more critical of Mozart admirers, for I distinguish in my mind between the merely workaday beautiful and the uniquely beautiful among his works. (I can even complain a bit, if properly encouraged, about the inordinate length of some of the operas.) I like Mozart best when I have the sensation I am watching him think. The thought processes of other composers seem to me different: Beethoven grabs you by the back of the head and forces you to think with him; Schubert, on the other hand, charms you into thinking his thoughts. But Mozart's pellucid thinking has a kind of sensitized objectivity all its own: one takes delight in watching him carefully choose orchestral timbres or in following the melodic line as it takes flight from the end of his pen.

Mozart in his music was probably the most reasonable of the world's great composers. It is the happy balance between flight and control, between sensibility and self-discipline, simplicity and sophistication of style that is his particular province. By comparison Bach seems weighted down with the world's cares, Palestrina otherworldly in his interests. Composers before him had brought music a long way from its primitive beginnings, proving that in its highest forms the art of music was to be considered on a par with other strict disciplines as one of man's grandest achievements.

Mozart, however, tapped once again the source from which all music flows, expressing himself with a spontaneity and refinement and breath-taking rightness that has never since been duplicated.

Berlioz Today

BERLIOZ IS THE ARCHETYPE of artist who needs periodic reappraisal by each epoch. His own period couldn't possibly have seen him as we do. To his own time Berlioz was an intransigent radical; to us he seems, at times, almost quaint. Wystan Auden once wrote: "Whoever wants to know the nineteenth century must know Berlioz." True enough, he was an embodiment of his time, and because of that I can't think of another composer of the past century I should have more wanted to meet. And yet, enmeshed in his personality are stylistic throwbacks to an earlier time; these tend to temper and equivocate the impression he makes of the typical nineteenth-century artist.

His biographer, Jacques Barzun, claims that one rarely finds a discussion of Berlioz "which does not very quickly lose itself in biographical detail." Berlioz is himself partly responsible for this because he wrote so engagingly about his life. Moreover, there is the fabulous life itself: the tireless activity as composer, critic, and conductor; the success story of the country doctor's son who arrives unknown in the big city (Paris) to study music and ends up, after several tries, with the Prix de Rome; the distracted and distracting love affairs; the indebtedness due to the hiring of large orchestras to introduce his works; the fights, the friends (Chopin, Liszt, De Vigny, Hugo), the triumphal trips abroad, the articles in the *Journal du Débat*, the *Mémoires*, and the bitter experiences of his last years. No wonder that in the midst of all this the music itself is sometimes lost sight of.

Admirers and detractors alike recognize that we are living in a period of Berlioz revival. Formerly his reputation rested upon a few works that remained in the orchestral repertoire: principally the *Symphonie Fantastique* and some of the overtures. Then came repeated hearings of *Harold in Italy, Romeo and Juliet,* and the *Damnation of Faust.* Recordings have made *L'Enfance du Christ* and *The Trojans* familiar; even the *Nuits d'Été* are now sung. Perhaps before long we may hope to hear unknown works like the *Song of the Railroads* (1846) or *Sara the Bather* (1834).

What explains this recent concern with the Berlioz *oeuvre?* My own theory is that something about his music strikes us as curiously right for our own time. There is something about the quality of emotion in his music—the feeling of romanticism classically controlled—that reflects one aspect of present-day sensibility. This is allied with another startling quality: his ability to appear at one and the same time both remote in time and then suddenly amazingly contemporary. Berlioz possessed a Stendhalian capacity for projecting himself into the future, as if he had premonitions of the path music was to take. By comparison, Wagner, in spite of all the hoopla surrounding his "music of the future," was really occupied with the task of creating the music of his own period. And yet, by the irony of musical history, Berlioz must have seemed old-fashioned to Wagner by the 1860's.

By the end of the century, however, it was clear that the French composer had left a strong imprint on the composers who followed after him. A study of *Harold in Italy* will uncover reminders of the work of at least a dozen late-nineteenth-century composers—Strauss, Mahler, Moussorgsky, Rimsky-Korsakoff, Grieg, Smetana, Verdi,

Tchaikovsky, Saint-Saëns, Franck, Fauré. (Nor should we forget the impact he had on his own contemporaries, Liszt and Wagner.) How original it was in 1834 to give the role of protagonist to a solo instrument—in this case a viola—and create, not a concerto for the instrument, but a kind of obbligato role for which I can think of no precedent. The line from *Harold* to *Don Quixote* as Strauss drew him is unmistakable. The second movement of *Harold in Italy* has striking similarities to the monastic cell music in *Boris Godounoff*, with all of Moussorgsky's power of suggestibility. Indeed, the history of nineteenth-century Russian music is unthinkable without Berlioz. Stravinsky says that he was brought up on his music, that it was played in the St. Petersburg of his student years as much as it has ever been played anywhere. Even the Berlioz songs, now comparatively neglected, were models for Massenet and Fauré to emulate. Nor is it fanciful to imagine a suggestion of the later Schönberg in the eight-note chromatic theme that introduces the "Evocation" scene from the *Damnation of Faust*.

When I was a student, Berlioz was spoken of as if he were a kind of Beethoven *manqué*. This attempted analogy missed the point: Beethoven's nature was profoundly dramatic, of course, but the essence of Berlioz is that of the *theatrical* personality. I once tried to define this difference in relation to Mahler—who, by the way, bears a distinct resemblance to Berlioz in more than one respect—by saying that "the difference between Beethoven and Mahler is the difference between watching a great man walk down the street and watching a great actor act the part of a great man walking down the street." Berlioz himself touched on this difference in a letter to Wagner when he wrote: "I can only paint the moon when I see her image reflected at the bottom of a well." Robert Schumann must have had a similar idea when he said: "Berlioz, although he often . . . conducts himself as madly as an Indian fakir, is quite as sincere as Haydn, when, with his modest air, he offers us a cherry blossom." This inborn theatricality is a matter of temperament, not a matter of insincerity. It is allied with a love for the grand gesture, the naïve-heroic, the theatric-religious. (In recent times Honegger and Messiaen have continued this tradition in French music.) With Berlioz we seem to be watching the artist watching himself create rather than the creator in the act, pure and simple. This is different in kind from the picturesqueness of Beethoven's *Storm* in the *Pastoral Symphony*. Berlioz was undoubtedly influenced by Beethoven's evocation of nature, but his special genius led to the introduction of what amounted to a new genre—the theatric-symphonic, and there was nothing tentative about the introduction.

The fact that Berlioz was French rather than German makes much of the difference. Debussy said that Berlioz had no luck, that he was beyond the musical intelligence of his contemporaries and beyond the technical capacities of the performing musicians of his time. But think of the colossal bad luck to have been born in a century when music itself belonged, so to speak, to the Germans. There was something inherently tragic in his situation—the solitariness, and the uniqueness of his appearance in France. Even the French themselves, as Robert Collet makes clear, had considerable trouble in fitting Berlioz into their ideas of what a French composer should be. In a sense he belonged everywhere and nowhere, which may or may not explain the universality of his appeal. In spite of Berlioz's passionate regard for the music of Beethoven and Weber and Gluck, it is the non-German concept of his music that gives it much of its originality.

This can perhaps be most clearly observed in his writing for orchestra. Even his earliest critics admitted his brilliance as orchestrator. But they could hardly have guessed that a century later we would continue to be impressed by Berlioz's virtuoso handling of an orchestra. It is no exaggeration to say that Berlioz invented the modern orchestra. Up to his time most composers wrote for the orchestra as if it were an enlarged string quintet—none before him had envisaged the blending of orchestral instruments in such a way as to produce new combinations of sonorities. In Bach and Mozart a flute or a bassoon always sounds like a flute or a bassoon; with Berlioz they are given, along with their own special quality, a certain ambiguity of timbre that introduces an element of orchestral magic as a contemporary composer would understand it. The brilliance of his orchestration comes partly by way of his instinctual writing for the instruments in their most grateful registers and partly by way of his blending of instruments rather than merely keeping them out of each other's way. Add to this an incredible daring in forcing instrumentalists to play better than they knew they could play. He paid the price of his daring, no doubt, in hearing his music inadequately performed. But imagine the excitement of hearing in one's inner ear sonorities that had never before been set down on paper. It is the sheen and sparkle, the subtle calculation of these masterly scores that convince me that Berlioz was more, much more, than the starry-eyed romantic of the history books.

It is easy to point to specific examples of Berlioz's orchestral boldness. The use of the double-basses in four-part chordal pizzicatti at the beginning of the *March to the Scaffold*; the writing for four tympany, also in chordal style, at the conclusion of the movement that precedes the *March*; the use of English horn and piccolo clarinet to typify pastoral and devilish sentiments respectively; the gossamer texture of *Queen Mab* with its impressionist harp and high antique cymbals; the subtle mixtures of low flutes with string tone at the beginning of the "Love Scene" from *Romeo*—all these and numerous other examples demonstrate Berlioz's uncanny instinct for the sound stuff of music.

Apart from his orchestral know-how there is hardly a phase of his music that has not been subjected to criticism. His harmonic sense is said to be faulty—that's the reproach most frequently heard—his structure too dependent on extramusical connotations, his melodic line disappointingly old-fashioned. These oft-repeated strictures are now due for revision. Any clumsiness in the handling of harmonic progressions should be viewed in the light of our extended notions of right and wrong in harmonic procedures. The Berlioz harmony admittedly is sometimes stiff and plain, but is it so awkward as to disturb one's over-all enjoyment? That always has seemed an exaggerated claim to me. His formal sense is unconventional —refreshingly so, I would say, for even when he lacks the inevitability of a Beethoven, one senses that he is finding his own solutions arrived at from his own premises. More often than not these are unexpected and surprising. The reproach concerning his melodic writing has some basis in fact, especially for the present-day listener. Berlioz depends upon the long-breathed line and the unconventional phrase length, to sustain interest, rather than the striking interval or pregnant motive. His loveliest melodies give off a certain daguerreotype charm, redolent of another day. This must have been true even at the time he penned them. Looked at from this angle, they lend his music a quite special *ambiance*, as if they came from a country not to be found on any map.

Let us concede, for the sake of argument, that the weaknesses are there. The fact remains that, whenever a composer is adjudged worthy to stand with the masters, a remarkable willingness to overlook what was formerly considered to be serious weaknesses is apparent. The weaknesses remain, but public opinion tacitly agrees to accept them for the sake of the good qualities—and I consider that public opinion does right. My prognostication is that we shall, in future, be hearing less and less of

Berlioz's weaknesses and more and more of his strengths.

For I repeat that there is something strangely right about Berlioz for our time. The French historian Paul Landormy put my meaning well when he wrote: "His art has an objective character by comparison with the subjectivity (intériorité) of a Beethoven or a Wagner. All the creatures that he created in his imagination detach themselves from him, take on independent life, even if they are only an image of himself. The Germans, on the contrary, have a tendency to fuse the entire universe with their interior life. Berlioz is essentially a Latin artist." It is the objective handling of romantic elements that makes Berlioz an especially sympathetic figure in our own time. That and our clear perception of his musical audacity. For he is clearly one of the boldest creators that ever practiced the art of musical composition.

An aura of something larger than life-size hangs about his name. After hearing a Berlioz concert Heinrich Heine wrote: "Here is a wing-beat that reveals no ordinary song-bird, it is a colossal nightingale, a lark as big as an eagle, such as must have existed in the primeval world."

Liszt as Pioneer

EVERYBODY THINKS he has the right to an opinion about Franz Liszt and his music. I can only recommend my own opinion tentatively because I admit to being dazzled by the man. As a composer, he has for me something of the same glamour he had for his contemporaries as pianist. His wizardry at the piano so overwhelmed audiences in his own day that they were clearly incapable of judging him soundly as a creator.

The question is whether anyone can do that even now. To examine his list of compositions, if only superficially, is enough to give one a dizzy feeling. It would be a feat merely to listen consecutively to the prime examples of his production: the symphonies, symphonic poems, concertos, oratorios, the masses, the chamber music, the songs, the piano compositions large and small, not to mention the plethora of fantasies, arrangements, and transcriptions of the works of numerous other major and minor composers. How can anyone be expected to arrive at a balanced, critical estimate of such a man?

Nevertheless I freely confess to being won over, so to speak, in advance. There is something endlessly diverting about a musician who, like Berlioz, was to such a degree the embodiment of his period. After all, the nineteenth century, especially the Lisztian part of it, was the "juiciest" period in music. One needn't be a composer of the greatest ability in order to mirror the times most truthfully. Quite the contrary. Chopin, for example, was perhaps too elegant, Mendelssohn too polite, and Schumann too sweetly honest to reflect the seamier side of their epoch. It's from Liszt that one gets a sense of the fabulous aspect of that era.

His composer friends, Chopin and Schumann, despite their appreciation of the Hungarian's genius, thought Liszt a rather shocking figure; they accused him of cheapening their art—and I suppose the accusation is not without justification. (One must remember, however, that he outlived both of them by more than a quarter of a century, and neither of them could have known the compositions that interest us most.) But the point is that what shocked them in Liszt is the very thing that fascinates us. It fascinates us because the qualities that Liszt had in abundance—the spectacular style, the sensuosity, the showmanship, the warmth and passion of his many-sided nature—are exactly those qualities that are least evident in contemporary music. No wonder he intrigues us, and in a way that only one or two other musical figures of the nine-teenth century can match.

There is another aspect of Liszt's personality that en-dears him to us. I am thinking, of course, of the enthusi-asm expended upon the compositions of other composers, many of them young and obscure when first he came to know their work. Genius, as a rule, is too self-concentrated to waste much time on lesser men. But in Liszt we have the rule's exception. With rare perceptivity he was able to sense the mature composer in the embryonic stage. And this interest in the output of his colleagues, which un-doubtedly had its origin in a character trait, in the end took on larger significance than Liszt himself may have realized. The French critic G. Jean-Aubry offers a good case for having us believe that it was Liszt who engen-dered one of the most important of recent historical developments: the rise of nationalism as a musical ideal. "If modern Germany had a profound sense of justice," writes Jean-Aubry, "she would nourish a vigorous hatred for Liszt, for the destruction of German musical monopoly is in part his work." In a period when Brahms and Wagner were at the apogee of their careers, and in spite of Liszt's well-known championship of Wagner, Liszt was clear-headed enough to understand that new music could ad-vance only if the hegemony of German music were weak-ened. To remember that fact makes one keenly aware of the forward-looking character of Liszt's own music.

The most advanced aspect of his own music is its harmonic daring. But, leaving this aside for the moment,

I would say that the element that strikes one most forcibly, separating his music from that of all other nineteenth-century composers, is its sonorous appeal. A keen ear will detect wide divergencies in "sound-pleasure" in the works of different composers. Laymen tend to take these divergencies for granted. But actually the type of sonorous appeal we take so much for granted—the sonority chosen instinctively for its sheer beauty of sound—is partly the invention of Liszt. No other composer before him understood better how to manipulate tones so as to produce the most satisfying sound texture ranging from the comparative simplicity of a beautifully spaced accompanimental figure to the massive fall of a tumbling cascade of shimmering chords. One might legitimately hold that this emphasis upon the sound-appeal of music weakens its spiritual and ethical qualities. Perhaps; but even so one cannot deny Liszt the role of pioneer in this regard, for without his seriously contrived pieces we would not have had the loveliness of Debussy or Ravel's textures or the langorous poems of Alexander Scriabine.

These essentially new sonorities were first heard at Liszt's piano recitals. The profusion of his works and their variety of attack are without parallel in piano literature. He quite literally transforms the piano, bringing out, not only its own inherent qualities, but its evocative nature as well: the piano as orchestra, the piano as harp (*Un Sospiro*), the piano as cimbalom (*Hungarian Rhapsody No. 11*), the piano as organ, as brass choir, even the percussive piano as we know it (*Danse Macabre*) may be traced to Liszt's incomparable handling of the instrument. These pieces were born *in* the piano; they could never have been written at a table. (It is indicative that an intellectual leader of his generation, Ferruccio Busoni, famous composer and pianist in his own right, should have spent many years in preparing the definitive edition of Liszt's piano compositions.) The display, the bravura, the panache of Liszt's piano writing—all this has been pointed out many times before, even a hundred years ago; the remarkable thing is that it has remained as true now as it was then.

On an equivalent plane of freshness and originality was Liszt's harmonic thinking. Even professional musicians tend to forget what we owe to Liszt's harmonic daring. His influence on Wagner's harmonic procedures has been sufficiently stressed, but not his uncanny foreshadowing of the French impressionists. One set of twelve piano pieces, rarely if ever performed, *L'Arbre de Noël*, and especially *Cloches du soir* from that set, might be mistaken for early Debussy. It is typical that although *L'Arbre de Noël* was written near the end of a long life it shows no lessening of harmonic invention. The scope of that invention can be grasped if we turn from the lush sonorities of another evening piece, *Harmonies du soir*, to Liszt's oratorio *Christus*. Here we enter an utterly opposed harmonic world, related to the bare intervallic feeling of the Middle Ages and the non-harmonic implications of Gregorian chant—startling premonitions of the interests of our own time. Throughout the length and breadth of Liszt's work we are likely to come upon harmonic inspirations: unsuspected modulations and chordal progressions touched upon for the first time. Moreover, his sense of "spacing" a chord is thoroughly contemporary: bell-like open sonorities contrasting sharply with the crowded massing of thunderous bass chords. It is not too much to say that Liszt, through his impact upon Wagner and Franck and Grieg and Debussy and Scriabine and the early Bartók, and especially the nationalist Russians headed by Moussorgsky, is one of the main sources of much of our present-day harmonic freedom.

I have left to the last Liszt's boldest accomplishment: the development of the symphonic poem as a new form in musical literature. The symphonic poem, as such, has had but a puny progeny in recent years. Composers look upon it as old-fashioned, *démodé*. But we mustn't forget that in Liszt's day it was a burning issue. To the defenders of classical symphonic form it appeared that a kind of theatrical conspiracy, spearheaded by Berlioz and seized upon by Liszt and Wagner, was about to seduce pure music from its heritage of abstract beauty. The new hotheads, taking their keynote from Beethoven's *Egmont Overture*, and *Pastoral Symphony*, insisted that music became *more* meaningful only if it were literary in inspiration and descriptive in method. The programmatic approach took hold: from the literal treatment of romantic subject matter in the Liszt-Berlioz manner the idea was both broadened and narrowed to include the poetic transcription of natural scenes as in Debussy's *La Mer*, or the down-to-earth bickerings of marital life as in Strauss's *Domestica*. By the early 1900's it looked as if the classical symphony were to be discarded as an old form that had outlived its usefulness.

As it turned out, it is the traditional form of the symphony that is still very much alive, and the symphonic poem that is in the discard. But strange to say, this does not invalidate the importance of Liszt's twelve essays in that form, for their principal claim to historical significance is not in the fact of their being symphonic poems but in their structural novelty.

Here once again we see the Hungarian's freedom from conventional thinking, for he was the first to understand that descriptive music should properly invent its own form, independent of classical models. The problem, as Liszt envisioned it, was whether the poetic idea was able to engender a new form—a *free* form; free, that is, from dependence upon formulas and patterns that were simply not apposite to its programmatic function. Form in music is a continuing preoccupation for composers because they deal in an auditory material that is by its very nature abstract and dangerously close to the amorphous. The development of type forms such as the sonata-allegro or fugue is a slow process at best; because of that, composers are naturally reluctant to abandon them. Liszt was a pioneer in this respect, for he not only relied on the power of his own instinctual formal feeling to give shape to his music, but he also experimented with the use of a single theme and its metamorphoses to give unity to the whole fabric. Both parts of Liszt's idea have deeply influenced contemporary music. The numberless sonatas that are not really sonatas but approaches to a freer form take their origin in Liszt's famous B-minor piano sonata; and the twelve-tone school itself, with its derivation of entire operas from the manipulation of a single "row," owes its debt to the pioneering of Franz Liszt.

Am I being too generous to old Abbé Liszt? If so, it is a generosity that is long overdue. Liszt has been the victim of a special stupidity of our own musical time: the notion that only the best, the highest, the greatest among musical masterworks is worthy of our attention. I have little patience with those who cannot see the vitality of an original mind at work, even when the work contains serious blemishes. For it would be foolish to deny that Liszt's work has more than its share of blemishes. How could he have imagined that we would not notice the tiresome repetitions of phrases and entire sections, long and short; the reckless overuse, at times, of the thematic material; the tasteless rehashing of sentimental indulgences? He was not beyond the striking of an attitude, and then filling out the monumental pose with empty gestures. He seems entirely at his ease only in a comparatively restricted emotional area: the heroic, the idyllic, the erotic, the demonic, the religious. These are the moods he evokes time after time. Moreover, he seemed capable of coping with no more than one mood at a time, juxtaposing them rather than combining and bringing them to fruition.

No, Liszt was not the perfect master. I will go so far as to admit that there are days when he seems quite intolerable. And then? And then one comes upon something like the two movements based on Lenau's *Faust* and is bowled over once again by the originality, the dramatic force, the orchestral color, the imaginative richness that carries all before it. The world has had greater composers than this man, no doubt, but the fact remains that we do him and ourselves a grave injustice in ignoring the scope of his work and the profound influence it has exerted on the contemporary musical scene.

Fauré Centennial in America: 1945

DURING THE LAST four days of November 1945, Cambridge, Massachusetts, is to be turned into a shrine for Fauré devotees. The Harvard Music Department is sponsoring a festival of five concerts, free to the public, in honor of the hundredth anniversary of the great French composer's birth. The music will range from the comparatively familiar *Requiem* through less familiar cham-

ber music and songs to the rarely performed opera
Pénélope, to be given in concert form under the direction
of Nadia Boulanger.

It is a little difficult for those of us who have long
admired Fauré's work to foresee how the present dwellers
in Harvard Yard will take to him. Personally I'm just a
trifle nervous. It isn't that one's faith in the value of the
work itself has wavered, but the moment doesn't seem to
be quite right for doing full justice to a Fauré celebration.
In a world that seems less and less able to order its affairs
rationally Fauré's restraint and classic sense of order may
appear slightly incongruous. Consequently it is only reasonable to speculate as to how he will "go over," especially
with younger listeners.

As a matter of fact, it has never been easy to convince
the musical public outside France of the special charm
that attaches itself to Fauré's art. In France itself Fauré's
name has for many years been coupled with that of Debussy, as is proper. But outside France the public has been
slow to appreciate his delicacy, his reserve, his imperturba-
ble calm—qualities that are not easily exportable.

It is perfectly true that you must listen closely if you
would savor the exquisite distinction of Fauré's harmonies
or appreciate the long line of a widely spaced melodic arch.
His work has little surface originality. Fauré belongs with
that small company of musical masters who knew how to
extract an original essence from the most ordinary musical
materials. To the superficial listener he probably sounds
superficial. But those aware of musical refinements can-

not help admire the transparent texture, the clarity of
thought, the well-shaped proportions. Together they con-
stitute a kind of Fauré magic that is difficult to analyze
but lovely to hear.

The public at large, when it knows his work at all,
knows it, as Theodore Chanler has pointed out, "through
a mere handful of works, all written before his forty-fifth
year." But Fauré lived to the ripe age of seventy-nine
and composed his most mature works during the last
thirty-five years of his life. It is the bulk of this later work
that is so little known, and undeservedly so. A song cycle
like *La Chanson d'Ève* belongs with the *Dichterliebe* of
Schumann; the second piano quintet belongs with
Franck's essay in that form; the piano trio should be heard
along with Ravel's trio.

At the age of sixty-seven Fauré wrote his first and
only opera, *Pénélope*. From a musical standpoint this
opera will stand comparison with Debussy's *Pélleas et
Mélisande*. Dramatically it suffers from an obviously weak
libretto, but despite that fact it continues to be performed
regularly in Paris. It is these works of his maturity—and
other similar ones—that arouse my enthusiasm.

I don't suppose that it is primarily the enthusiast
like myself at whom the centenary concerts are aimed.
And, of course, the sponsors of the festival must know
that there are people of good will who will continue to
think of Fauré as a *petit maître français* no matter what
one demonstrates to the contrary. Assuming that they
really know Fauré's music—not just the early violin sonata

and some of the songs, but the ripe works of his maturity
—they have a right to their opinions. But what about the
many music lovers who have never had an opportunity
of forming their own opinions? Certainly the festival must
have been devised with them in mind—for the true be-
liever in the genius of Fauré is convinced that to hear
him is to love him.

4· FROM A COMPOSER'S JOURNAL

LA FORME FATALE

It seems to me now that there are two kinds of composers of opera. This thought occurred when I heard Henry Barraud explain his reluctance to plunge into a second opera after the performance of his first, *Numance*, at the Paris Opéra. His hesitation rang a bell and echoed my own thoughts. The fact that we can reasonably balance the thought of the labor and possible returns of an opera and decide calmly whether to launch into one again indicates that we are both different from the composer who is hopelessly attached to this *forme fatale*. We *play* at writing operas, but the operatic repertory is made up of works by men who could do little else: Verdi, Wagner, Puccini, Bizet, Rossini. It is some consolation to recall that we have precedent among the great dead who "played at it" too: *Fidelio*, *Pelléas*, *Pénélope*. (Mozart is, as always, a law unto himself.)

RAVEL AS ORCHESTRATOR

Georges Auric tells me that Ravel said to him that he would have liked to write a brochure on orchestration, illustrated by examples from his own work that did *not* come off. In other words, the reverse of Rimsky-Korsakoff's treatise, in which he illustrates only his successes. Auric also claims that Ravel told him he was dissatisfied with the final orchestral crescendo of *La Valse*. When I told this to Nadia Boulanger, she said that the morning after the première of *Bolero* she called to compliment Ravel on the perfection of his orchestral know-how. She reports that Ravel replied rather sadly, "If only the *Chansons madécasses* had come off as well." Curious, isn't it, that this humble approach to the arcana of instruments combined should be the mark of the virtuoso orchestrator. (Schönberg quotes Mahler and Strauss to the same effect.)

THE SOIGNÉ APPROACH

If there is anything more deadly to musical interpretation than the *soigné* approach, I don't know what it is. (Thought of this during X's concert last night.) When the emphasis is all on sheen, on beauty of sound, on suavity and elegance, the nature of the composer's expressive idea goes right out the window. Composers simply do not think their music in that way. Before all else, they want their music to have *character*—and when this is all smoothed away by removing the outward marks of personality—furrowed brow and gnarled hands and wrinkled neck—we get nothing but a simulacrum of beautiful (in themselves) sonorities. When that happens in a concert hall, you might as well go home. No music will be made there that night.

COMPOSER REACTIONS

Nothing pleases the composer so much as to have people disagree as to the movements of his piece that they liked best. If there is enough disagreement, it means that everyone liked something best—which is just what the composer wants to hear. The fact that this might include other parts that no one liked never seems to matter.

MUSIC AND THE MAN OF LETTERS

The literary man and the art of music: subject for an essay. Ever since I saw Ezra Pound turn pages for George Antheil's concert in the Paris of the twenties, I have puzzled over what music means to the literary man. For one thing, when he takes to it at all, which is none too often, he rarely seems able to hear it for itself alone. It isn't that he sees literal images, as one might suspect, or that he reads into music meanings that aren't there. It's just that he seldom seems *comfortable* with it. In some curious way it escapes him. Confronted with the sound of music, we are all mystified by its precise nature, and react differently to that mystery: the medical doctor has an easy familiarity with it, often using it as a means of moving back quickly to the world of health; the mathematician looks upon it as the sounding proof of hidden truths still to be uncovered; the minister utilizes it as handmaiden in the Lord's work . . . But the literary man, he seems mostly to be uncomfortable with it, and when he puts two words together to characterize a musical experience, one of them is almost certain to be wrong. If he uses an adjective to describe a flute, it is likely to be the one word a musician would never connect with the flute. A recent quotation from the letter of a dramatist: "If there is incidental music in the play, it should sing on the romantic instruments and forswear brass and tympany.[!]" For one G.B.S. or one Proust or one Mann there are dozens of literature's great who rarely if ever venture a mention of music in the length and breadth of their work. These are the wise ones; the others, gingerly stepping amid the notes, are likely to fall flat on their faces. These others are the ones who puzzle me—and arouse a benign and secret sympathy.

COMPOSER PSYCHOLOGY

At lunch with Poulenc, who recounted at great length the libretto of his new opera, *Les Dialogues des Carmélites*. It was easy to see how much the fate of this work, still to be heard, means to him. A little frightening to contemplate what his disappointment will be if the opera doesn't "go over." And yet he is giving it to La Scala of Milan for its world première—La Scala, famous for making mincemeat of new operas. There is something very composerish about all of this, for we would all willingly put our heads into the same noose. (Postscriptum: Poulenc won out this time!)

IN BADEN-BADEN

Today I was reminded of my intention to write someday an orchestral work entitled *Extravaganza*. It seems a long long time since anyone has written an *España* or *Bolero* the kind of brilliant orchestral piece that everyone loves.

THE ORCHESTRAL MUSICIAN

Conducting the Sudwestfunk Orchestra, a particularly intelligent bunch of musicians, put me in mind of how curious a creature the typical orchestral musician is. Being the underdog in a feudal setup, he quickly develops a sort of imperturbability, especially as regards music. One can almost say that he flatly refuses to get excited about it. He is being paid to do a job—"Now let's get on with it, and no nonsense about it" is the implied attitude. You cannot play an instrument in an orchestra and admit openly a love for music. The rare symphonic instrumentalist who has managed to retain his original zest for music generally finds some means for expressing it outside his orchestral job. In thirty years of back-stage wandering I have never yet caught a musician with a book on music under his arm. As for reading program notes about the pieces he plays, or attending a lecture on the aesthetics of music—all that is unthinkable.

Something is wrong somewhere. Someone must find a way to make of the orchestral performer the self-respecting citizen of the musical community he would like to be.

FILM SCORES

The touchstone for judging a Hollywood score: Was the composer moved in the first instance by what he saw happening on the screen? If there is too much sheen, he wasn't; if there are too many different styles used, he wasn't; if the score is over-socko, he wasn't; if the music obtrudes, he wasn't. It is rare to hear a score that strikes one as touching because of the fact that the composer himself was moved by the action of the film.

SCHONBERG AS INTERPRETER

I once heard *Pierrot Lunaire* conducted by its composer. It was a revelation of the value of understatement in interpretation—an element in interpretation that is little discussed nowadays. I was reminded of this by a quotation from Richard Strauss on the subject of his heroine Salome: "Salome, being a chaste virgin and an oriental princess, must be played with the simplest and most restrained of gestures. . . ." Schönberg underplayed the inherent hysteria of his lunar Pierrot—normalized it, so that it took its place alongside other musics instead of existing as the hysterical-musical curiosity of a tortured mind.

TEMPI

Of all the subtle qualities needed by a conductor, none is more essential than an instinct for adopting correct tempi. A gifted band of musicians can, if need be, balance itself (at least in repertory works); the solo instruments can project satisfactorily on their own; stylistic purity can be achieved naturally—but with the flick of a wrist a conductor can hurry a movement needlessly, drag a movement interminably, and in so doing distort formal lines, while the orchestra plays on helplessly. Conductors, in matters of tempi, are really on their own. Composers rarely can be depended upon to know the correct tempo at which their music should proceed—they lack a dispassionate heartbeat. The proof is simple: Ask any composer if he believes his own freely chosen metronome marks are rigidly to be adhered to, and he will promptly say, "Of course not." A composer listening to a performance of his music when the pacing is inept is a sorry spectacle indeed! He may be unable to set the right speed but he certainly can recognize the wrong one.

VOICES

I hate an emotion-drenched voice.

THE YOUNG CONDUCTOR

After watching young student conductors for many years at Tanglewood I have decided that few things are more difficult than to judge adequately young talent in the conducting field. On the other hand, observing them at work helps to clarify what conducting really is. No man has the right to stand before an orchestra unless he has a complete conception in his mind of what he is about to transmit. In addition, he must possess a natural and easy authority, one that imposes itself without effort on each player. Without a conception there is, of course, nothing to impose. If one adds to this a natural facility of gesture, and a certain dramatic flair, then the visual aspect is taken care of. One needs, besides, an infallible ear, plus the ability to feel at home in many different styles. No wonder the student conductor often presents a pitiful spectacle. He cannot know, until it is put to the test, whether he has the right to be standing where he stands. But by the time he reaches the podium, it is too late. Unless he has "the gift," he is in for a rough time. Few experiences can be so unnerving; and at the same time, few successes more genuinely rewarding.

MUSICAL AROUSAL

In a certain mood reading about music can excite one at the prospect of hearing some in rather the same way that reading about sex arouses one's lubricity.

GENIUS IN A SMALL WORLD

It takes a long time for a small country to get over a great man—witness Finland and Sibelius. Norway has taken fifty years to get over Grieg, and it looks as if Denmark would need as long a time to get beyond Carl Neilsen. If I were any of these men, it would not make me happy to know that my own work engendered sterility in my progeny.

The Twenties and the Thirties: How It Seemed Then

1. THE YOUNGER GENERATION
OF AMERICAN COMPOSERS:
1926—59

Prefatory Note: A reading of these three articles in chronolo-
gical sequence should provide some perspective on the unfolding of America's creative talent during the past thirty
years. Through no fault of my own several late-comers are
not named: Walter Piston in the twenties, William Schuman
in the thirties, and Leon Kirchner in the forties. They are
missing because their music was little known until a later
time. George Gershwin, on the other hand, was famous in
1926, but was down in everyone's book as a composer of
popular music with only two concert pieces to his credit.
Most significant, it seems to me, is the fact that the writing
of articles such as these has become increasingly hazardous
due to the variety and complexity of our present-day musical
scene.

1926: *America's Young Men of Promise*

To DISCOVER the important composers of tomorrow among the young men of today has always proved a fascinating diversion. Franz Liszt, in his time, concerned himself with every rising young talent in Europe who happened to cross the path of his meteoric career. More recently Erik Satie played godfather to a whole brood of young Frenchmen. Braving ridicule, he even sought among the high-school boys for young genius. Others beside Satie have gathered about them the significant young men—Busoni and Schönberg in Central Europe, Casella in Italy.

In America our new composers have been left to shift for themselves. When, as occasionally happens, a young talent does emerge from obscurity, this can almost always be attributed to the sensational element in his work, never to its purely musical merits. The public wants only a name. But there are other composers, less fortunate, who must be content to add opus to opus with little or no hope of being performed. If these cannot be heard, they can at least be heard about. Perhaps hearing about them may induce someone to let us really hear them.

This is not intended to be a complete presentation of the youngest generation of composers in America. I have simply chosen seventeen names among those men, born here, whose ages lie between twenty-three and thirty-three, whose music has seemed to me to be worthy of special note. Not that this is, in any sense, a critical estimate of their work. It is too soon for that. But it does indicate a promising group of young men whose compositions deserve consideration. For convenience, these seventeen names might be grouped as follows:

Four Prix de Rome men: Leo Sowerby, Howard Hanson, Randall Thompson, G. Herbert Elwell.

Three revolutionaries: George Antheil, Henry Cowell, Roger Sessions.

Five free-lances: Roy Harris, Avery Claflin, Edmund Pendleton, Richard Hammond, Alexander Steinert.

Three pupils of Ernest Bloch: Bernard Rogers, W. Quincy Porter, Douglas Moore.

Two pupils of Nadia Boulanger: Virgil Thomson, Quinto Maganini.*

Of the first four, recipients of the American Prix de Rome, at least two, Leo Sowerby and Howard Hanson, are too well known to need introduction. The same cannot

---

* It is interesting to note that the subsequent importance of Mademoiselle Boulanger as teacher of American composers was not yet apparent.

be said, unfortunately, of either Randall Thompson or G. Herbert Elwell.

Randall Thompson (1899), after three full years in Rome, has but recently returned to this country. His preliminary training at Harvard and a year under Bloch have given him a firm grasp of the materials of composition. He writes with ease in all forms. His most mature works, written in Rome, include choral settings for *Seven Odes of Horace* (three with orchestral accompaniment); *Piper at the Gates of Dawn* for orchestra; a piano sonata and suite, and a string quartet.

Each one of Thompson's compositions is finished with a most meticulous pen—not an eighth note that does not receive full consideration before it is put on paper. For the moment this very excellence of workmanship seems to be offered in lieu of a more personal style. While Thompson never borrows outright from any one composer, it is not difficult to detect the influence of certain Europeans, Pizzetti, Bloch, Stravinsky, in the several movements of a single work. Thus far Thompson's *Ode to Venice*, for chorus and orchestra, and especially his string quartet are the works in which he seems nearest to the achievement of a personal idiom.

In G. Herbert Elwell, now residing at the Academy in Rome, we have a young composer who will not long remain the unknown quantity he is in American music. Elwell is no conventional winner of prizes. He has spent the last five years in Europe—London, Paris, Rome— living life his own way. In 1919 he came to New York from Minneapolis to study composition with Ernest Bloch and continued later in Paris under Nadia Boulanger during the years 1922–24.

Even Elwell's earliest student work had stamped upon it the distinct mark of his own individuality. That individuality is most easily recognized in his scherzo movements, an elflike quality, not of delicacy and charm, but of sharp quips and puckish fancies. His music is dynamic, muscular, alive—weakest, perhaps, in its lyrical moments. There have been passing influences of Rimsky-Korsakoff, Dukas, Bloch, but these need cause us no great concern. With every new work his art becomes more ripe.

Elwell has written much for the piano—a sonatina, a sonata, nine short pieces. His *Quintet* for piano and strings is being presented in Paris this spring. The *Centaur* for orchestra (1924) and his most recent work, a ballet based on Max Beerbohm's *Happy Hypocrite*, complete the list of his compositions.

It is a sign of health that we in America also have our radicals in the persons of George Antheil, Roger Sessions, Henry Cowell. For one reason or another their names have been bruited about, though their music has remained more or less inaccessible here.

George Antheil, the most notorious of the trio, must by now be weary of hearing himself called the *enfant terrible* of American music. Antheil's fame first spread among his literary fellow-countrymen in Berlin and Paris. These expatriates were none too careful of their superlatives. Potentially speaking, Antheil is all they claim and more; one needn't be particularly astute to realize that he possesses the greatest gifts of any young American now writing. No one can venture to dictate just how he may make the best use of his great talents; one can simply remark that so far the very violence of his own sincere desire to write original music has hindered rather than helped the attainment of his own ends.

Antheil's latest work, with its use of numerous mechanical pianos and electrical appliances, takes on the aspect of visionary experiment. This is probably a passing phase. He is still under twenty-five; the next few years will give the true measure of his importance.

Of Roger Huntington Sessions I can speak only from hearsay. No example of his work has been given publicly in the larger music centers, yet the high opinions of his music held by Ernest Bloch and Paul Rosenfeld command respect. Up to the spring of 1925 he acted as Bloch's assistant in Cleveland, which in part explains his very small output. A work that has aroused much comment is his incidental music to Andreyev's play, *The Black Maskers*. He is at present in Florence, devoting his entire time to composition.

Henry Cowell has hardly suffered from lack of publicity. He has presented programs of his music from coast to coast and throughout the Continent, even in districts as remote as Poland. He has written much for the piano and for small groups of instruments. Like Schönberg, Cowell is a self-taught musician, with the autodidact's keen mind and all-inclusive knowledge.

But Cowell is essentially an inventor, not a composer. He has discovered "tone clusters," playing piano with the forearm, and the string piano. Yet from a purely musical standpoint his melodies are banal, his dissonances do not "sound," his rhythms are uninteresting. Cowell must steel himself for the fate of the pioneer—opposition and ridicule on the one hand, exploitation and ingratitude on the other. His most interesting experiments have been those utilizing the strings of the piano. The *Banshee*, when performed in a small room, is musical noise of a most fascinating kind. Perhaps if Cowell develops along these lines he may even make a distinctive path for himself as composer.

Something of the variety of American life and its effect upon musicians as compared with the usual conservatory product of Europe can be seen in the destinies of three young men of twenty-seven—Avery Claflin, Roy Harris, and Edmund Pendleton. They have but little music to their credit, yet each one writes from an absolute inner necessity that forces its way out in spite of material obstacles.

Avery Claflin, a New Englander by birth, had most of his musical training in Boston and at Harvard. The war brought him to France, where he remained for a year after the armistice, during which time he had contact with the Cocteau-Satie group. He is at present connected with a bank, so that his time for composition is strictly limited. His works are quickly listed: a one-act opera on an adaptation of Edgar Allan Poe's *Fall of the House of Usher*,

147

a trio, a chorus for male voices, and several songs. Claflin does not write with great freedom; he seems somewhat hampered by a lack of facility in composing. This does not detract, however, from the simple charm of certain episodes and the inherent musical quality in all his work.

Roy Harris, a Californian, possesses a talent that should be carefully nurtured. Until a few years ago he was engaged in one form or another of manual labor so that he is seriously handicapped by his late start in music. But on the other hand he was born with a full-fledged style of his own. Harris is a child of nature with a child's love for his native hills and a childlike belief in the moral purpose of music. His music reflects these things faith-fully—it owes nothing to city influences, but seems always full-blooded and spiritually pure. His melodies and, even more particularly, his harmonies are in no way revolution-ary, yet they have a strangely personal flavor. Harris has written very little, his most ambitious undertaking being six movements for string quartet and two movements of an incomplete *Symphony* for large orchestra.

It is difficult to supply much information concerning Edmund Pendleton. In the spring of 1924 I heard an orchestral work by this young composer at the Salle Gaveau in Paris. In spite of the apparent influence of Stra-vinsky this one work placed Pendleton among the promis-ing young men of today. He has lived abroad for more than five years now, studying at one time under Eugene Cools, the French composer. A more recent orchestral composition, *When the Circus Comes to Town*, had its première in Paris in the fall of 1925.

Richard Hammond is a composer who cannot be easily classified. Except for short pieces his works are rarely performed in public. He studied for several years with Mortimer Wilson and his major compositions comprise a *Suite of Six Chinese Fairy Tales* for orchestra, a sonata for oboe and piano, several song cycles with the accompaniment of orchestra or piano, and numerous piano pieces.

Due to insufficient information about the work of Alexander Steinert, a talented young composer of Boston, I have been unable to do more than include his name here.

It is surprising, to say the least, to note the number of these young men who have profited by the teachings of Ernest Bloch or Nadia Boulanger or both. Bernard Rogers has the distinction of being Bloch's first pupil in America. He is not unknown in these parts, several of his compositions, *To the Fallen*, a *Prelude to The Faithful*, *Soliloquy* for flute and string orchestra, have been presented by major organizations. America possesses few composers with Rogers' seriousness of purpose. He is an idealist, a dreamer—New York, his native city, repels him with its crass materialism. His music is sensitive, poetic, carefully made, even though for the present it lacks the imprint of a pointedly individual style. He has recently completed a new score, *Japanese Impressions*, and is now at work on a symphony.

Both Douglas Moore and W. Quincy Porter have emerged from the same background, the Yale School of Music and, later, Bloch. At present Moore is in Paris on a Pulitzer scholarship. I can speak of his work only from hearsay. His two suites for orchestra, *Museum Pieces* and *P. T. Barnum*, are said to contain pages of rare humor.

Since 1922, W. Quincy Porter has been teacher of theory at the Cleveland Institute of Music. Like Hindemith, Porter is a first-class viola player and has accordingly written much for strings. A *Ukrainian Suite*, for string orchestra, and two string quartets comprise his major works. All these are characterized by an especially fine mastery of contrapuntal technique and an easy handling of the problems of form. But unfortunately they are largely derivative in inspiration—Stravinsky and Bloch in the quartets; Russian masters in the *Suite*. Porter is not yet thirty, he has chosen fine models, we can confidently await his more mature development.

Of Nadia Boulanger's pupils two should be singled out for special mention—Virgil Thomson and Quinto Maganini. Virgil Thomson, besides composing, writes uncommonly well about music. His academic training was at the Harvard School of Music, from which he was graduated in 1922. There is much that is paradoxical in his music. It is generally of two kinds, diametrically opposed to each other: sacred vocal music like the *Mass* for men's voices, *Three Antiphonal Psalms* for women's voices, songs for voices and piano on biblical texts; and on the other hand, tangos for orchestra and light pieces for piano. At its best his work displays a melodic invention of no mean order and a most subtle rhythmic sense growing out of a fine feeling for prosody. Certainly Thomson has not entirely found himself as yet. One waits with more than usual curiosity to see what he will do in the future.

Quinto Maganini, despite the Italianate sound of his name, is a native American, brought up in California. A large part of his knowledge of composition has been gained in a practical way as flautist in symphonic orchestras. Though not yet thirty, Maganini has a considerable list of works to his credit. He has traveled extensively and is strongly attracted by local color, so that one finds him writing a *Fantasy Japonaise*; *La Rumba de Monteagudo*, based on Cuban popular music; *Tuolumna*, for orchestra, with a suggestion of Indian themes. A symphonic nocturne, *Night on an Island of Fantasy*, is perhaps his most successful effort in the larger forms. With a more critical pen Maganini should make one of our promising composers.

The day of the neglected American composer is over. That is to say, he is neglected only if he remains unknown. These seventeen young men are presented as proof of the fact that there is a new generation of composers whose efforts are worthy of encouragement.

1936: America's Young Men—
Ten Years Later

"AMERICA'S YOUNG MEN OF PROMISE"
was the title of an article that may be remembered as
having appeared just ten years ago. Seventeen composers
were boldly chosen—all of them born here, ranging in age
from twenty-three to thirty-three—as most likely to ac-
complish important things in American music. With
bated breath let me relist the composers I named, leaving
it to the reader to decide whether they were wisely chosen.
Among those present were George Antheil, Avery Claflin,
Henry Cowell, Herbert Elwell, Howard Hanson, Roy
Harris, Richard Hammond, Quinto Maganini, Douglas
Moore, Edmund Pendleton, Quincy Porter, Bernard
Rogers, Roger Sessions, Alexander Steinert, Leo Sowerby,
Randall Thompson and Virgil Thomson.

My purpose in bringing out this list again is two-
fold: first, to reconsider these composers in the light of a

decade of activity on their part, and, second, to juxtapose a new list of "America's Young Men of Promise," since discovering the "important composers of tomorrow among the young men of today" is still as fascinating a diversion as it was in 1926.

The first question that suggests itself is whether that original band of seventeen did represent a real generation of American composers. I think that it did. Perhaps it is not too much to say that they represented the most important generation of composers America had yet produced. Originating in all parts of the country, they nevertheless shared many experiences in common: student days before and during the war years, European contacts made soon after 1919, followed by a busy period of creative activity during the healthy, hectic years of the twenties. By 1926 their main characteristics as composers were already discernible.

In general they were technically better equipped and more aware of the idiom of their contemporaries than any preceding generation of Americans. None of them suffered from the folkloristic preoccupation of their elders with Indian and Negro thematic material. Still, the idea of expressing America in tone was uppermost. Yet they seemed no more able than their predecessors to forge a typically indigenous American style in music.

For purposes of identification these seventeen men can now be described as roughly falling into four different categories: Those who have made a more or less sudden rise to prominence since 1926; those who have continued to compose along the same lines in a steady, unwavering fashion; those who have remained in comparative obscurity; and those who have abandoned composing altogether.

I make no claim to being familiar with every piece of music written by each of these men since 1926. Nor is it my purpose to criticize the single work of any individual composer. What appears interesting is to examine their present status in the light of a decade of experience and activity; to check up, as it were, on their progress during the past ten years.

In the first category mentioned above belong Roy Harris, Virgil Thomson, and, in a lesser degree, Roger Sessions. The case of Roy Harris is probably most striking. His admirers and detractors are already legion. I do not belong among those who seem satisfied with continually pointing out his weaknesses. Without in any way wishing to condone them, I believe that the work he has already done, stamped as it is with the mark of a big personality, is something to build on, something we can ill afford to treat slightingly. Harris's music shows promise of being able to reach a very wide audience, wider probably than that of any other American. His name is already almost analogous with "Americanism" in music. This is a rather remarkable record for one who was not only completely unknown ten years ago, but who was, musically speaking, practically inarticulate. For Harris the problem of being fully articulate still remains. When he solves that, all barriers will be down between himself and his audience.

Virgil Thomson needs no introduction to my readers.

The success of *Four Saints* came as a surprise certainly, but on second thought seems quite natural. For Thomson is a composer who knows exactly what he wants. *Four Saints* is thoroughly characteristic of his work as a whole. In it he proves himself to be essentially a vocal composer. As I have pointed out on other occasions, Thomson is the first American whose sense of the English language seems really acute. His vocal line is based on the rhythmic flexibility and natural inflection of human speech, and may well serve as a model for future composers.

In contrast with Harris and Thomson, Roger Sessions has achieved slowly but surely a wide reputation both as a composer of serious works and as a musician of solid culture. In 1926 we took it on the word of Bloch and Paul Rosenfeld that Sessions was a musical radical. But now it is clear that Sessions is really the classicist par excellence. The small number of his works make up in quality what they lack in quantity. Sessions' music cannot be expected to appeal to large audiences—in a certain sense he writes a musician's music, intent as he is upon achieving a plastic and formal perfection, with little regard for audience psychology. His influence as composer and pedagogue will surely be felt increasingly.

Randall Thompson and Bernard Rogers have both gradually been making their mark on American music. Thompson, particularly, enjoys a well-deserved reputation as an expert craftsman. It is curious to observe how a man of Thompson's scholarly interest and academic background has come to make a definite bid for popular appeal, as in his *Symphony No. 2* Thompson has the audience very much in mind when he composes. This attitude is not without its dangers, particularly when the composer gives us the impression, as Thompson sometimes does, that he has been concentrating on the sonorous effect rather than the musical thought behind it.

Bernard Rogers has composed much in the past few years. But since none of his major works has been performed outside of Rochester, where he makes his home, I cannot speak authoritatively about them.

Recently Quincy Porter's name has come to the fore through his string quartets and his sonata for viola alone. Porter has turned out a considerable number of works, especially for stringed instruments, since my first article appeared. These are so gratefully written for the strings that it would be strange if they did not become better known. But Porter's essential problem still remains—to create a music entirely his own.

In speaking of the second category—composers who have continued more or less along the same lines they had adopted before 1926—I had in mind such varied personalities as Hanson, Sowerby, Cowell, and Moore.

Hanson and Sowerby were well launched even ten years ago. Their sympathies and natural proclivities make them the heirs of older men such as Hadley and Shepherd. Their facility in writing and their eclectic style produce a kind of palatable music that cannot be expected to arouse the enthusiasm of the "elite," but does serve to fill the role of "American music" for broad masses of people.

Cowell remains the incorrigible "experimenter" of

the twenties. In 1926 I wrote: "Cowell is essentially an inventor, not a composer."* I must regretfully still subscribe to that opinion, despite the ingenuity of such inventions as his *Synchrony* for orchestra.

Douglas Moore early showed a predilection for making use of an American subject matter as a basis for his work. After *P. T. Barnum* we got *Moby Dick* and *Babbitt*. Unfortunately these works have been too infrequently played for us to know whether the music is as American as the titles.

Four of the original seventeen composers—Hammond, Claflin, Maganini, and Steinert—have receded into comparative obscurity.** This is possibly less true of Steinert, whose works are performed from time to time. He has with difficulty extricated himself from a definitely impressionistic bias. Hammond, Claflin, and Maganini have written much music during the past ten years but very little of it has been played. Can this be simply a matter of neglect or is it the fault of the music itself?

Two composers have apparently stopped composing altogether: Herbert Elwell and Edmund Pendleton. Both, however, lead active lives as musicians and writers on music: Pendleton in Paris and Elwell in Cleveland as critic of the Cleveland *Plain Dealer*.***

George Antheil, as always, belongs in a category of

* This opinion needs revision in view of Cowell's eleven symphonies and other recent works.
** "Obscurity" cannot in justice describe the busy musical lives of Steinert, Claflin, and Maganini.
*** Both Elwell and Pendleton have resumed their composing careers along with their profession of music criticism.

his own. In 1926 Antheil seemed to have "the greatest gifts of any young American." But something always seems to prevent their full fruition. Whether this is due to a lack of artistic integrity, or an unusual susceptibility to influences, or a lack of any conscious direction, is not clear. All we know is that Antheil is now thirty-five, and we have a right to expect definitive works from him by this time.

Two or three composers should be mentioned who, because of their age, rightfully belong with the original group, but were omitted because they were unperformed before 1926.

First of these, and most important, is Walter Piston. His preparation for composing was obviously an arduous one. His earliest listed music, a Piano *Sonata*, is dated 1926, when Piston was thirty-two. Since then a steadily mounting number of works has been matched by a steadily increasing and well-merited reputation. Piston belongs with Sessions as one of the most expert craftsmen American music can boast.

A second and almost parallel case as far as dates are concerned is that of Robert Russell Bennett. His "first" work, written at the same date and age as Piston's, is a *Charleston Rhapsody* for orchestra. He is well known now as the composer of music that is light in touch and deftly made, with a particular eye on orchestral timbre, of which he is a past master.

William Grant Still began about twelve years ago as the composer of a somewhat esoteric music for voice and a few instruments. Since that time he has completely changed his musical speech, which has become almost popular in tone. He has a certain natural musicality and charm, but there is a marked leaning toward the sweetly saccharine that one should like to see eliminated.

Turning to the youngest composers of today one is immediately conscious that they find themselves in a quite different situation from that of the preceding generation. In a sense they form a "depression generation," for they live in a moral climate that is none too good for the nurturing of new talent. While opportunities for getting their work before the public have definitely increased, the public itself is apathetic to new music as a whole, showing a lack of interest toward the new men.

There seems to be no other explanation for the general impression that no especially outstanding personalities are to be found among the new men who are comparable in stature to the outstanding members of the preceding generation.

They can be conveniently divided according to age: Those who are just about twenty-five, and those who are either older or younger than twenty-five. The first group, which includes some of the most gifted men, is made up of Robert McBride, Jerome Moross, Paul Bowles, Hunter Johnson and Samuel Barber.

The older men, including some of the more mature talents, are Marc Blitzstein, Israel Citkowitz, Gerald

Strang, Ross Lee Finney, Elie Siegmeister, Irwin Heilner, Lehman Engel, Paul Creston, and Edwin Gershefski.

The youngest are: Henry Brant, David Diamond, and Norman Cazden.

A larger number of names will be familar than would have been true ten years ago. Marc Blitzstein's is probably best known. Blitzstein shows a definite "flair" for composition, although his early works were largely derivative (Stravinsky was the all-absorbing influence). Later, when he managed to throw off these influences, his music took on an exaggeratedly laconic and abstract quality, which militated against its even achieving performance. Recently, however, he has returned to a simpler style more nearly approaching the best parts of his early ballet *Cain*, or some of his film music for *Surf and Seaweed*. This new simplicity may be attributed to Blitzstein's sympathy for leftist ideology, with its emphasis on music for the masses.

The identification of one's musical aims with the needs of the working class is a brand-new phenomenon in American music. Young men like Siegmeister, Heilner, Moross, and Cazden have felt irresistibly drawn toward the movement to the left, which has influenced all other arts before reaching music. Unfortunately it cannot be said that their works show the salutary influence of a collectivist ideal. (This is not so strange when we consider that to compose a music of "socialist realism" has stumped even so naturally gifted a man as Shostakovitch.)

Siegmeister has had difficulty in adopting a real simplicity in his more serious works. Too often, as in his

Strange Funeral at Braddock, we get a kind of crude effectiveness, quite undistinguished in style. What is needed here is more honest self-criticism. Heilner is a naturally gifted composer, though he is given to extremes. He recently abandoned a highly complex tonal fabric, inspired no doubt by the examples of Ives, in order consciously to embrace banality. That idea for reaching the masses is literary and certainly will not satisfy a musician like Heilner for long.

Moross is probably the most talented of these men. He writes music that has a quality of sheer physicalness, music "without a mind," as it were. It is regrettable that we cannot yet point to any finished, extended work. What he seems to lack is a sense of artistic discipline and integrity, which his talent needs for development.

Norman Cazden, an excellent pianist, has recently been brought to our attention as the composer of a *Piano Sonatina* and a *String Quartet* that augur well for his future as a creative artist.

Of a completely different inspiration is the music of Citkowitz and Bowles. Both these men are lyricists and write an unmistakably personal music. Citkowitz, who is certainly one of the most sensitive and cultured musicians we have, has produced but little in the past few years. It is to be fervently hoped that the composer of such delicate and admirable pieces as the Joyce *Songs* and the *Movements for String Quartet* will soon get his second wind, and present us with works we have a right to expect from him.

Paul Bowles is the exceptional case among our young composers. There are those who refuse to see in Bowles anything more than a dilettante. Bowles himself persists in adopting a militantly non-professional air in relation to all music, including his own. If you take this attitude at its face value, you will lose sight of the considerable merit of a large amount of music Bowles has already written. It is music that comes from a fresh personality, music full of charm and melodic invention, at times surprisingly well made in an instinctive and non-academic fashion. Personally I much prefer an "amateur" like Bowles to your "well-trained" conservatory product.

If it is careful workmanship that is desired, turn to the music of Ross Lee Finney and Samuel Barber. Finney's music becomes more interesting with each new work. He composes largely in the neoclassic model, which produces a certain sameness that should be avoided in the future. Barber writes in a somewhat outmoded fashion, making up in technical finish what he lacks in musical substance. So excellent a craftsman should not content himself forever with the emotionally conventional context of his present manner.*

Three composers—Engel, Brant, and Diamond—are extremely prolific and facile. Facility brings its own pitfalls, of course. To compose easily is admirable, but the music must always spring from a deep need. Neither

* Written when Mr. Barber was twenty-six. He must have arrived at a similar conclusion, if one can judge by the sophisticated style of his more mature music.

Engel nor Brant, despite self-evident musicality, has yet completely convinced us that each is "hopelessly" a composer. David Diamond is a new name on the roster of young composers. It is a name to remember. Not yet twenty-one, Diamond has a musical speech that is, of course, only in the process of formation. But already one can recognize an individual note in his last-movement rondos with their perky, nervous themes and quick, impulsive motion.

Robert McBride has also but recently made his metropolitan bow. Those who heard his *Prelude to a Tragedy*, performed by Hans Lange and the Philharmonic, were greatly impressed. McBride's orchestral sense is both keen and original. Being himself a performer on several orchestral instruments, he approaches the whole problem of composing from a more practical standpoint than is general among our young men, who too often find themselves divorced from direct contact with the materia musica. McBride has yet to learn how to purify his style of extraneous elements, and how to create a feeling of inevitability in the musical thought. Still, no composer during the past few years has made so fresh an impression on first acquaintance.

Finally there are the young men whose names are little known: Strang of California, Johnson of the Middle West, Gershefski of Connecticut, and Creston, a native New Yorker. It is a characteristic sign that they are all composers of excellent training. In general, however, their work has a disturbing tendency toward overcomplexity of texture and a somewhat abstract musical thought. There is a certain unreality about their music, which probably comes from their lack of contact with a real audience. Perhaps it is wrong to generalize about four such different personalities. Strang's music has been little played outside his native state. All the others have recently had evenings of their work at the WPA Forum Laboratory Concerts and will undoubtedly profit by their experiences there.

In 1946 we shall know more about all these men.

1949: The New 'School' of American Composers

WHEN I WAS IN MY TWENTIES I had a consuming interest in what the other composers of my generation were producing. Even before I was acquainted with the names of Roy Harris, Roger Sessions, Walter Piston, and the two Thom(p)sons, I instinctively thought of myself as part of a "school" of composers.

Without the combined effort of a group of men it seemed hardly possible to give the United States a music of its own.

Now—and how soon, alas—my contemporaries and I must count ourselves among the spiritual papas of a new generation of composers. But personally I find that my interest in what the young composers are up to is just as keen as it ever was. For it is obvious that you cannot set up a continuing tradition of creative music in any country without a constant freshening of source material as each decade brings forth a new batch of composers.

It seems to me that one of the most important functions of those who consider themselves guardians of musical tradition, particularly in our Western Hemisphere, where the creative musical movement is still so young, is to watch carefully and nurture well the delicate roots of the youngest generation; to see to it that they get a sound musical training, that their first successful efforts are heard, and that they feel themselves part of the musical movement of their country.

In the United States young composers appear to be sprouting everywhere. My impression is that we are just beginning to tap our creative potentialities. The generation of the 1930's—Marc Blitzstein, William Schuman, Samuel Barber, David Diamond, and Paul Bowles—is now well established. The generation of the 1940's—with which this article is concerned—is being encouraged with prizes, commissions, fellowships, money grants, and, more often than not, performances of their works. Nowadays, in this country at any rate, a young composer with exceptional talent would have a hard time escaping detection.

Unlike the composers of my own generation, most of these younger men have not (as yet) been to Europe. In a very real sense Europe has come to them, for many of them have had personal contact with Stravinsky, Hindemith, Schönberg, Milhaud, and Martinu, all of whom are living and composing in the United States.* It would be strange indeed if the presence of these contemporary masters had no effect whatever on our younger generation.

But added to this influence by way of Europe there is a new note: our young composers follow closely the work of their older American colleagues. My own generation found very little of interest in the work of their elders: MacDowell, Chadwick, or Loeffler; and their influence on our music was nil. (We had only an inkling of the existence of the music of Charles Ives in the twenties.) Nowadays a young American composer is just as likely to be influenced by Harris or Schuman as he is by Stravinsky or Hindemith. (Perhaps, to fill out the picture, I should add that numbers of them have been accused of writing like me!)

In general, the works of the youngest generation reflect a wide variety of compositional interests rather than any one unified tendency. In the United States you can pick and choose your influence. Of course, we also have our twelve-tone composers, most of them pupils of Krenek or Schönberg, even though they have not yet played much

* 1949.

of a role. All this would seem healthy and natural, given the particular environment of our musical life and the comparatively recent development of our composing potential.

But enough of generalities. I have chosen seven names as representative of some of the best we have to offer among the new generation: Robert Palmer, Alexei Haieff, Harold Shapero, Lukas Foss, Leonard Bernstein, William Bergsma, John Cage. Most of these composers either are just approaching thirty or have just passed thirty. (Foss is the youngest of the group, having only recently turned twenty-four.) They are all native-born Americans, with the exception of Haieff and Foss, both of whom came to the United States at the age of fifteen and were musically formed here. All of them are composers of serious works that have been publicly performed and, occasionally, published and recorded.

Robert Palmer is perhaps the least well known of this group. He is also one of the oldest—thirty-two. His music is seldom heard in ordinary concert life: most of it found its way to public performance on special modern-music programs or at annual festivals of American music. Palmer happens to be one of my own particular enthusiasms. I remember being astonished ten years ago when I first saw him, and tried to make some connection in my mind between the man and his music. His outward appearance simply did not jibe with the complexities of the metaphysical music he was writing at that time.

Ives and Harris were his early admirations, to which

he added his own brand of amorphous transcendentalism. Later he came under the sway of Bartók's rhythmic drive. Two string quartets represent him at his best. They are lengthy works, not easy to perform, and not easy for the listener to digest.

But both quartets contain separate movements of true originality and depth of feeling. Palmer is not always as critical as he should be, especially in the outlining of the general proportions of a movement, but always his music has urgency—it seems to come from some inner need for expression.

In two recent works, an orchestral *Elegy for Thomas Wolfe* and a sonata for two pianos, he has managed to discipline the natural ebullience of his writing, though sometimes at the expense of a too rigid polyrhythmic or melodic scheme. Palmer may never achieve the perfect work, but at least he tries for big things. In recent years too much of his energy has gone into his teaching at Cornell University, but teaching is a familiar disease of the American composer. Thus far in his career Palmer has enjoyed little public acclaim; nevertheless, if he has the capacity to endure and to develop, his future seems to me assured.

Alexei Haieff was born in Russia and brought up in China, but had his musical education under Rubin Goldmark in the United States. Later he studied in Paris under Nadia Boulanger. His background and training give him a strong affinity with the music of Stravinsky, and, in fact, Haieff is a close personal friend of that master. Stravinsky's shadow was pervasive in his earlier works, but gradually Haieff has emerged with a sharply defined personality of his own. He combines a sensitive and refined musical nature with an alert musical mind that often gives off sparks of mordant humor. He delights in playful manipulation of his musical materials, and has a special fondness for sudden interruptions of the musical flow with abrupt silences or unexpected leaps or brief backtrackings.

Thus far Haieff has composed few large and imposing works. Although he has written a *First Symphony*, he seems most at home in his shorter pieces such as his *Divertimento* for chamber orchestra, *Sonata* for two pianos, *Five Pieces for Piano*, and other short works for violin and piano or cello and piano. Almost all of these pieces are a musical pleasure—they have personality, sensibility, and wit. They divert and delight the listener, not in a superficial sense but in the sense that such terms might be applied to a Couperin or a Scarlatti. Haieff is at present engaged in the composition of a long ballet based on *Beauty and the Beast*, to be choreographed by George Balanchine for the Ballet Society of New York. It will be interesting to see how he handles a large canvas.

Harold Shapero, it is safe to say, is at the same time the most gifted and the most baffling composer of his generation. This young Bostonian, now twenty-seven, has a phenomenal "ear" and a brilliant (though sometimes erratic) mind. The ear and the mind were subjected to a methodical training under Krenek, Piston, Hindemith, and Boulanger. These teachers left their mark; Shapero now possesses an absolutely perfected technical equipment.

To examine one of his scores closely is a fascinating experience. Few musicians of our time put their pieces together with greater security either in the skeletal harmonic framework, in the modeling of the melodic phrases, or in the careful shaping of the whole. Shapero knows what he's doing, but that is the least of it: the exciting thing is to note how this technical adroitness is put at the service of a wonderfully spontaneous musical gift. Despite this there is, as I say, something baffling about what he has produced thus far.

Stylistically Shapero seems to feel a compulsion to fashion his music after some great model. Thus his five-movement *Serenade for String Orchestra* (a remarkable work in many ways) is founded upon neoclassic Stravinskian principles, his *Three Sonatas for Piano* on Haydnesque principles, and his recent long symphony is modeled after Beethoven. For the present he seems to be suffering from a hero-worship complex—or perhaps it is a freakish attack of false modesty, as if he thought to hide the brillance of his own gifts behind the cloak of the great masters. No one can say how long this strange attitude will last. But when Shapero decides to make a direct attack on the composing problem, to throw away all models, and to strike out unconcernedly on his own, I predict the whole musical world will sit up and take notice.

Lukas Foss is, in a way, the *Wunderkind* of this group of composers, and something of the aura of the *Wunder-*

kind still hangs about him. Born in Berlin, where he had his first music lessons, he continued his studies at the Conservatoire in Paris during the Hitler years, and finally arrived in New York with his parents at the age of fifteen. At thirteen he had already composed piano pieces (subsequently published by G. Schirmer) that are almost indistinguishable from those of his later master, Hindemith.

The contact with America was crucial. In Europe he had acquired a kind of impersonal cocksureness that was not at all sympathetic. In America, as he grew up, he became more human and more anxious to reflect the atmosphere of his newly adopted country. His first large work of "American" inspiration was an oratorio, *The Prairie*, for soloists, chorus, and orchestra, with a text chosen from Carl Sandburg's indigenous poems. It was a striking work to come from the pen of a nineteen-year-old boy. Since then he has composed two long works for solo voice and orchestra—*Song of Protest* for baritone, and *Song of Songs* for soprano, both based on texts from the Bible.

I cannot honestly say that I always admire his treatment of the English language. But it is impossible not to admire the spontaneity and naturalness of his musical flow, the absolute clarity in texture, and the clean and easy handling of large formal problems. That Foss is a born composer is obvious.

William Bergsma is a native of California and a musical product of the Eastman School of Music in Rochester, New York. Hardly out of school himself, he already is one of the teachers of composition at the

Juilliard School. (William Schuman, head of the school, was quick to recognize Bergsma's sure craftsmanship.)

Bergsma is, by temperament, a sober and serious workman. I realize that this is not a very exact description of his particular talent, but it is difficult to say more at the present time, for the specific quality of his personality is not yet clear. He possesses a poetic and critical mind, and one is certain that his compositions are put together slowly, after mature reflection. Thus far he has composed orchestral and chamber music, songs, piano pieces, and a ballet. At this writing he is engaged upon a first symphony. How truly original or how broad in scope his music may turn out to be is a question for the future. But already it is clear from works like his two string quartets that Bergsma represents one of the solid values of the younger generation.

Leonard Bernstein's composing gift has been overshadowed by his brilliance as conductor and pianist. In a sense it would be strange if he could not compose, for his ability in that direction is only one of the various facets of an extraordinarily versatile musical personality. For us Bernstein represents a new type of musician—one who is equally at home in the world of jazz and in the world of serious music. George Gershwin made something of an attempt to fill that role, but Bernstein really fills it—and with ease.

Although his composing time is severely restricted by his activities as conductor, Bernstein has to his credit a symphony, *Jeremiah*; two ballets, *Fancy Free* and

Facsimile; a clarinet and piano *Sonata*, songs, and piano pieces.

The most striking feature of Bernstein's music is its immediacy of emotional appeal. Melodically and harmonically it has a spontaneity and warmth that speak directly to an audience. (After so much dissonant counterpoint and neoclassic severity this was a new note for a young composer to strike.) At its worst Bernstein's music is conductor's music—eclectic in style and facile in inspiration. But at its best it is music of vibrant rhythmic invention, of irresistible élan, often carrying with it a terrific dramatic punch. It is possible that some form of stage music will prove to be Bernstein's finest achievement. In general it is difficult to foretell the durability of music like Bernstein's, which is so enormously effective on first hearing.

I have saved for the last one of the curiosities of the younger generation: the music of John Cage. During the late twenties the experimental percussion music of Edgar Varèse and Henry Cowell made much noise among the musical *avant-garde*. Cage stems from there, much to the surprise of many of us who thought that the percussion period in modern music was definitely over.

Cage began in California with a percussion music of his own, obviously derived from that of his elders. But gradually he devolved the use of the so-called "prepared" piano as a percussive medium. A piano is "prepared" by inserting various metal and non-metal materials between the strings of the instrument. This produces a muted tone of delicately clangorous variety with no resemblance what-ever to piano tone. It must be heard to be appreciated—and it must be heard close by, for the tone is tiny and of little duration, somewhat like that of the harpsichord. But even music for prepared pianos must, in the end, be judged like other music.

Fascinating as it is, I fear that Cage's music has more originality of sound than of substance. Stylistically it stems from Balinese and Hindu musics, and more recently from Arnold Schönberg.

Serious music is thriving in the United States. One factor not often noted is the way our music schools and colleges are turning out composers in numbers unparalleled in our musical past. If we can gauge the musical future of a nation by the healthy activity of its younger generation of composers, then America is likely to do well.

The seven composers discussed in this article are near the top of the heap, but in many ways they are typical of their generation. They are all well-trained musicians and, what is more, American-trained. Their works show influences, of course. But it is a sign of the times that those influences are no longer solely European, for the older generation of American composers has helped to orient them.

It is also typical that they can knock out all sorts of music: a successful ballet like Leonard Bernstein's *Fancy Free*; a big oratorio like Lukas Foss's *Prairie*; a real symphony like Harold Shapero's; expert string quartets like those of William Bergsma or Robert Palmer; unusual forms like the piano music of John Cage; delightful shorter pieces like those of Alexei Haieff.

These young men don't form a "school" in a stylistic sense. But they all write music that is rhythmically alive, richly melodic, and clearly conceived. I believe that, taken altogether, these representative seven men and their colleagues throughout the country form an impressive group —one that need not fear comparison with the younger generation of any other country. That is something new for America.

1959: Postscript for the Generation of the Fifties

IN MY PREFATORY NOTE to the three preceding articles on American composers I mentioned the variety and complexity of our creative musical scene of today. It is a question whether anyone can hope to summarize the work of the generation of the fifties. One would have to live simultaneously in the four corners of the U.S.A. to know what is going on. There are so many composers active in so many parts of the country that no one observer can pretend to know them all. To take one instance: for every one opera written during the twenties there must be twenty being composed nowadays; and comparable figures are true for other musical media.

Nevertheless, if we leave aside the large mass of competent and average music that is always being produced, and concentrate on the ambitious compositions of our more adventurous composers, certain tendencies are discernible. The most striking one is the return, since 1950, to a preoccupation with the latest trends of European composition. This comes as a surprise, for, from the standpoint of their elders, it is retrogression of a sort. It is retrogression because it places us in a provincial position *vis-à-vis* our European confreres. The older generation fought hard to free American composition from the dominance of European models because that struggle was basic to the establishment of an American music. The young composer of today, on the other hand, seems to be fighting hard to stay abreast of a fast-moving post-World War II European musical scene. The new continental composer of the fifties began by re-examining the twelve-note theories of Arnold Schönberg in the light of their more logical application by Anton von Webern. From there he proceeded to a music of total control and its opposite, the music of chance and the music of non-simultaneity, with side forays into the fascinating world of electronically produced sounds, their mixture with normal music, and so forth. All this stirred things up considerably, especially since these young leaders of musical thought abroad—

Pierre Boulez in France, Karlheinz Stockhausen in Germany and Luigi Nono in Italy—have found sponsors and publishers to back them, instrumentalists—and this is important—willing to struggle with their pyrotechnical difficulties, and audiences willing to take them on faith. They created what we in America would call a workable setup.

Our own youngsters have been less successful in that regard. They have not managed thus far to create a world in which they can fully function as composers. They have been encouraged by awards and fellowships, but their music has not been furthered by conductors on the lookout for new things, and only an occasional performer has ventured to perform their music in public. Such circumstances can be frustrating in the extreme, and it is hard to see where they can possibly lead. That such a cul-de-sac is far from inevitable is proven by the fact that John Cage and his followers have developed audience support and press interest with music that is no less experimental in nature.

One might point also to the example of Elliott Carter, who has shaped a music of his own out of a wide knowledge of the music of our time. His theories concerning metrical modulation and structural logic have engaged the attention of our younger composers. Their own music, however, lacks similar directional drive. I detect in it no note of deep conviction: they seem to be exploring *possible* ways of writing music suggested to them by the example of composers abroad rather than creating out of their own experience and need a music that only they could write.

I am, of course, generalizing, which is always a dangerous thing to do. Already some youngster may be giving the lie to my reasonings. Even within the area I have outlined we have young talents whose music commands attention: Billy Jim Layton, Salvatore Martirano, Seymour Schiffrin, Edward Miller, Yehudi Wyner, Kenneth Gaburo, and the young Robert Lombardo. A composer like Gunther Schuller has asserted his independence by calling for a cross-fertilization of improvised jazz with contemporary serious music. His own music seems born out of a striking instrumental imagination; later on he may fill it out with a musical substance that matches the fascination of his sonorities. Easley Blackwood, who was a musical rebel in his teens, has developed along conservative lines a music that is arresting. Surprisingly few younger composers belong in that category, but one might add the names of Noël Lee and Mordechai Sheinkman.

Many of the questions that puzzled the generation of the twenties are still being asked today. What kind of music ought we to visualize for a future America? What form should it take? To whom shall it be addressed? Obviously our younger men will work out their own solutions without asking our advice. But it is only natural that we should hope that they will be able to find sustenance in the answers we found for the music of our own time.

2. EUROPEAN FESTIVALS AND PREMIÈRES: A GLANCE BACKWARD

═══════════

Zurich: 1926

ONE NOTED WITH REGRET at the fourth festival presented by the International Society for Contemporary Music, last June in Zurich, that no name entirely unfamiliar appeared on any of the six programs. In 1923 and 1924 a more adventurous spirit prevailed. Were undiscovered talents more numerous or were juries more perspicacious? In any event, this year's jury seemed quite content simply to offer a list of names that looked impressive, without concerning itself overmuch about the quality of the music played. If we were spared a great bore, we were also vouchsafed no revelations. The programs had an even, safe tone that augurs none too well for future festivals.

Of equal significance is the fact that no one work proved an outstanding success this year; but there was, so to speak, an outstanding failure—the Arnold Schönberg

Quintet for Wind Instruments. Seldom has a new work from the pen of a composer of wide repute suffered such universal condemnation. Except for certain parts of the scherzo and the final rondo, there seemed to be nothing but principles and theories of composition leading to complete aridity. The Schönberg disciples, however, are undismayed. Mr. Anton von Webern assures me that one has no more reason to expect to appreciate this *Quintet* on a single hearing than to understand Kant after a cursory perusal. This sounds good enough to make us hope that there is truth in it, even though our musical sensibilities remain sceptical.

As usual, the majority of compositions performed came from the French and German contingents. The juxtaposition of their works made clear once again the different ideals that actuate the composers of these countries. The young Frenchmen are inspired by the example of Chabrier and Fauré, the young Germans by that of Reger and Mahler. With these backgrounds it is curious to note that at the latest festival the Germans, with Hindemith, Webern, and Petyrek, made the better showing.

Paul Hindemith was represented by his *Concerto for Orchestra*, Opus 38, one of his latest and best works. Like Balzac, Hindemith possesses a healthy, robust talent. Mere notes mean nothing to him, it is the spirit that matters. That is to say, he is capable of taking common melodies, trite rhythms, tasteless harmonies, and by sheer temperament combined with a formidable technical equipment, transfuse them into something completely irresistible. It is an extraordinary vigor and exuberance, as demonstrated in this *Concerto*, that has singled Hindemith out as the most promising composer of young Germany. No less remarkable—but less remarked by the critics—is the peculiar beauty of his quiet episodes, a searching, wistful, hopeless quality such as we find in the earlier song cycle *Das Marienleben*.

How different an art from Hindemith's is that of a supersensitive musician like Anton von Webern. Where one writes four pages, the other writes four measures. That these *Five Orchestral Pieces* had been written as long ago as 1913 seemed almost incredible. One listens breathlessly: each piece lasts but a few seconds and each separate note seems filled with meaning. Most striking of all is Webern's orchestration—a subtle mingling of single timbres producing a magical result.

Less well known in America is Felix Petyrek, who contributed a *Litanei* for mixed chorus, two trumpets, harp, and percussion. It is an extremely effective work; there is much brilliant writing for the voices and at no time does the composition drag. Petyrek has to his credit a long list of works; we should like to hear more of them.

The French ranged against these men Caplet, Ferroud, and Hoerée. *Le Miroir de Jésus* is undoubtedly André Caplet's most noteworthy accomplishment, yet a foreigner cannot consider it, as they do in Paris, a masterpiece. It seems, rather, like Scriabine's *Prometheus*, a *chef d'oeuvre manqué!* Its qualities are obvious: the atmosphere of purity and restraint, the liquid harmonies, the original melodic line; and yet it too patently lacks variety to leave us with anything but a sense of monotony.

P. O. Ferroud is a native of Lyon, a pupil and ardent disciple of Florent Schmitt. His orchestral work, *Foules*, seemed rather amorphous and not particularly original. Arthur Hoerée of Brussels fared even less well with a *Septuor* for flute, string quartet, piano, and voice.

Two young men deserve special mention: Hans Krasa of Prague and William T. Walton of London. Krasa's two movements—*Pastoral* and *March*—taken from a symphony for small orchestra seemed more important when we heard them under Straram a few years ago in Paris, but they still are indicative of a brilliant gift. Walton's overture, *Portsmouth Point*, is gay and pleasant music, an English version of the "Back to Bach" style, with well-turned melodies and square-cut rhythms.

While Russia was inadequately represented by a second-rate piano sonata of Miaskowsky, Switzerland had contributions from two composers: a *String Trio* by Walter Geiser and Ernst Levy's *Fifth Symphony* in one movement. The Zurich public seemed to find the latter work rather long and tiresome. Levy is a metaphysical composer in the line of Beethoven and therefore, of course, hopelessly out of style. Nevertheless, this symphony seemed to come from a genuine urge and a keen ear could detect moments of real power and imagination.

Last, and probably least, was a *Concerto* for violin and woodwind orchestra by Kurt Weill, a young German.

The less said about this very dull work, the better, particularly since there seems to be a certain tendency to regard his more recent one-act opera, *Der Protagonist*, as quite important.

One leaves these festivals with the distinct impression that the music played is after all a secondary matter; but that an international meeting place is offered where the composers and other musicians of all countries may come together seems in itself invaluable.

Baden-Baden: 1927

THE FESTIVAL of *Deutsche Kammermusik*, which was inaugurated in 1921 at Donaueschingen under the patronage of Prince Max Egon zu Fuerstenberg, took place this year at Baden-Baden, a need for larger quarters making the change necessary. Five varied and engrossing programs were presented thanks to the perspicacity of a committee of three: Heinrich Burkard, Josef Haas, and Paul Hindemith. Two concerts of chamber music, an afternoon of original works for mechanical instruments, an evening of motion pictures with music, and finally a performance of four one-act chamber operas gave an excellent cross-section of music in 1927. Men of established reputations like Bartók and Berg rubbed elbows with young radicals like Kurt Weill. Even new talents were disclosed such as the twenty-four year old Russian, Nicolai Lopatnikoff.*

The festivals when formerly given at Donaueschingen differed from all others in that a new form was suggested to composers each year as a field for experiment. Thus compositions for small chorus in madrigal style were encouraged in 1925 and music for military band and for mechanical instruments in 1926. This policy was retained at Baden-Baden and the attention of composers was directed to chamber opera. Chamber opera is a growth from the recent widespread interest in chamber orchestra, the intention being not to write grand opera reduced to a small scale but to conceive a work directly for a few singers and a few instrumentalists. It was a delightful experiment, suggesting manifold possibilities, and the four little operas heard on the evening of July 17 proved unquestionably to be the event of the festival.

The shortest and best work, in my opinion, was Darius Milhaud's *opéra minute*, as he calls it: *The Abduction of Europa* on a libretto of Henri Hoppenot. The entire opera takes only eight minutes to perform. Milhaud, who understands the medium admirably, was

* Now an American citizen, professor of composition at Carnegie Institute of Technology.

the first to venture in this field and has already produced several small operas, notably *Les Malheurs d' Orhpée* and *Esther de Carpentras*. My own enthusiasm for this recent example of his work was not shared by many of its hearers at Baden-Baden. A renewed acquaintance with the vocal score, however, has only served to strengthen my conviction that it is a little *chef d'oeuvre*. Milhaud possesses one of the most personal styles of our day. In *The Abduction of Europa* he expresses the tender, nostalgic side of his nature in which a French sensuousness and elegance of melodic line is tinged by a Hebraic melancholy. The heavy-handed performance afforded the delicate work at Baden-Baden did much to obscure its very real merits.

The chamber opera that aroused most discussion was Kurt Weill's *Mahagonny* (accent on the third syllable, please!) A pupil of Busoni's, Weill is the new *enfant terrible* of Germany. But it is not so easy to be an *enfant terrible* as it used to be and nothing is more painful than the spectacle of a composer trying too hard to be revolutionary. Weill, in writing *Mahagonny*, cannot escape the accusation. It is termed a "*songspiel*" and is, in effect, a series of pseudo-popular songs in the jazz manner. (One remembers particularly Jessie and Bessie repeatedly singing in English, "Is here no telephone.") Weill is not without musical gifts, but these are too often sacrificed for the sake of a questionable dramatic effectiveness.

Hindemith's *Hin und Zurück* is based on a sketch from Charlot's Revue in which a little melodrama is played first forward and then backward with hilarious results. The music was also reversed, with Hindemith's customary mastery. Though not particularly remarkable for its musical content, *Hin and Zurück* proved a highly diverting piece.

The Princess on the Pea by Ernst Toch, after the fairy tale of Hans Andersen, was charming enough but did not avoid the pitfall of being grand opera on a small scale. Toch is a composer who has been gradually coming to the fore in Germany, but though he commands astonishing facility in the use of modern technique, his music seems to me essentially conventional.†

Of the works played at the two concerts of chamber music Alban Berg's *Lyric Suite* for string quartet found most favor. Unlike so many examples of this composer's output, the *Lyric Suite* is comparatively easy to comprehend. Perhaps this is due to the striking clarity of construction. It is in six well-contrasted parts, all of them frankly emotional, containing a lovely *andante amoroso*, and a shadowy and original *allegro misterioso*. Berg is now forty-two and it is foolish to continue discussing him merely as a Schönberg pupil. The similarities between his own style and that of his teacher's are only superficial. In reality their natures are opposed, Berg, unlike Schönberg, being essentially naïve, with a warm, emotional, Tristanesque personality. The *Lyric Suite* seems to me to be

† This statement needs revision in the light of the many works composed by Ernst Toch since 1927, especially his Pulitzer prize-winning *Symphony No. 3.*

one of the best works written for string quartet in recent years.

On the same program Béla Bartók played his own *Sonata for Piano*, composed in 1926. Nothing could be more characteristically Bartók than this sonata with its Hungarian folk tunes, its incisive rhythms, its hard, unsentimental quality. To possess so characteristic a manner carries with it the danger of self-repetition, and Bartók has come perilously near it in his sonata.

A first performance anywhere was given of a little cantata for a trio of women's voices, tenor, piano and violin, by Hanns Eisler. In comparison with the amusing and purposely banal text of the *Diary* the music seemed lacking in humor. Nevertheless it was apparent that this young pupil of Schönberg and Webern is more than usually gifted.

The afternoon devoted to mechanical music made clear that only music written expressly with the special problems of mechanical instruments in mind can be called entirely successful. This was well understood by Nicolai Lopatnikoff, one of the discoveries of the festival. His *Toccata* and *Scherzo* for mechanical piano combined astonishing *prestissimos* and other manually impossible feats with a freshness and originality of inspiration that reminded one of Prokofieff. A *Suite* for mechanical organ by Paul Hindemith was composed in his best manner. Ernst Toch also had a *Study* for mechanical organ. A garbled version of the first part of Antheil's *Ballet*

Mécanique was given with a badly functioning mechanical piano.

One word should be added about the music that Hindemith wrote for mechanical organ to accompany an animated cartoon called *Krazy Kat at the Circus*. The wit and *diablerie*, the abundant flow of melodic ideas, the vitality and force of this little commentary on a very amusing film confirmed one's opinion that in Hindemith Germany has its first great composer since 1900.

Paris: 1928

(ON STRAVINSKY'S "OEDIPUS REX")

· *Oedipus Rex* is Igor Stravinsky's most recent composition. Jean Cocteau made a new version of the Sophocles drama, which Stravinsky set as an opera-oratorio in two acts for a speaker, solo voices, male chorus, and orchestra. It was first performed last spring in Paris without stage action (as an oratorio) by the Russian Ballet. An audience that had come to be diverted by a spectacle and dancing was confronted with rows of singers in evening clothes who sang—none too well—an austere choral composition that proved far from amusing. Little wonder, then, that *Oedipus Rex* was coldly received. People on all sides could be heard regretting the old, familiar Stravinsky of *Le Sacre* and deploring what seemed to be an illogical *volte-face* on the part of the composer.

It is undoubtedly true that Stravinsky is no longer the composer *à la mode* of a few years back. This is due largely to the disfavor with which his latest manner, inaptly termed a "return to Bach," has been received. The conservatives call it a perverse mockery of classical models, while the modernists are reluctant to exchange the pleasurable jolts of a primitive period for the sober intellectualism of the *Concerto for Piano*.

Superficially, it does seem as if Stravinsky, possessed by the restless spirit of the age, felt impelled to invent a new style for each new work. Closer examination, however, reveals the complete unity of aesthetic purpose in all his production, from *Petrouchka* to *Oedipus Rex*. Already, in *Le Sacre du Printemps*, the primitive rites of an entire people are celebrated rather than the single tragedy of the puppet Petrouchka. The subjective realism of that earlier ballet was, in *Le Sacre*, tempered by a more impersonal spirit. Again, with *Les Noces*, there is the expression of a more objective realism, while in the last pages of the *Symphonies of Wind Instruments* the first signs of a complete break with realism become evident.

Thus, as Stravinsky progressed, he became more and

more enamored of the objective element in his creative work, until, about 1923, with the *Octet* he completely abandoned realism and espoused the cause of objectivism in music. This was no easy task he set himself. Music, more than any other art, has been profoundly influenced by the ideals of nineteenth-century romanticism. Even today the average musician confuses the term music with romantic music. It is easy for him to love and reverence the music of so-called classical composers like Bach and Palestrina. But it is another matter to admit that the impersonal attitude these men took toward their art might be applied as a living principle to present-day music.

It is just such an attitude that Stravinsky wishes to revive. It is more than likely that he was partly influenced by the example of a neoclassic Picasso. The reader of Clive Bell or T. S. Eliot will here recognize a tendency that has already manifested itself in modern painting and contemporaneous literature. But in music such aesthetic principles have not been alive for several centuries. With this in mind perhaps we can better appreciate the revolutionary gesture of Stravinsky in returning to the impersonal ideals of the eighteenth century.

With *Oedipus Rex*, Stravinsky applied the objective theory to the dramatic form. His wholehearted acceptance of tradition in this work is amazing; from every aspect—subject, form, action, rhythm, melody, etc.—he fearlessly started from the most banal premises. As subject matter he chose the universally known tragedy of King Oedipus. This was cast into the outmoded and restricted form of

the opera-oratorio as practiced by Handel. The action of
the opera remains static; in this manner the listener gets
no dramatic surprises: the singers comment on a *fait ac-
compli*. The text of the opera was translated from the
French of Cocteau into Latin, so that a dead language
might keep the listener's attention directed solely toward
tonal values.

From a purely musical standpoint *Oedipus Rex* is ex-
ternally made up of elements no less banal. Stravinsky,
the master of rhythmical complexities, has been content
to express dynamic intensity by the simplest means—
ordinary three-four, four-four rhythms. Harmonically,
also, there is marked restraint. After a welter of atonalisms
and polytonalisms, Stravinsky proposes a kind of unitonal
music in which there is almost no modulation, and where
for entire pages the harmony rests on a single major or
minor triad. The melodic line likewise remains close to
classical models. Creon sings *"Respondit deus"* to the
barest of progressions: a descending do-sol-mi-do-do. Old
formulas are brought to life in the general construction;
thus, Jocasta's solo is preceded by the usual recitative and
is followed by the conventional air—lento, allegro, lento.
Contrapuntally, as Arthur Lourié has pointed out,
Stravinsky has emulated Handel in that the counterpoint
is a resultant of the underlying harmonic structure rather
than a determinant of the harmony, as in the case of
Bach. Stravinsky's orchestration, likewise, shows admirable restraint. Although only the customary instruments
are employed, the prevailing timbre is hardly less new-

sounding than that derived from the special orchestration
—four pianos and percussion—of *Les Noces*.

To cope successfully with so many self-imposed
limitations, one must have the personality of a Stravinsky.
Yet it is not alone as a tour de force that *Oedipus Rex*
is remarkable. Its purely musical qualities far outshadow
its triumph over traditional means. The opening and clos-
ing pages of choral writing are magnificent. They have an
elemental force—a solidity and sobriety that Stravinsky
himself has seldom achieved. There is nothing clever or
ironic in this music. The broad majestic lines upon which
the score has been conceived bring a new note into modern
music. Such arias as that of Tiresias in the first act, or
the long solo of Jocasta with which the second act begins,
are profoundly human. Very characteristic of the new
Stravinsky are the crystalline trumpet calls that ring out at
the appearance of the messenger and the exciting chorus
that immediately follows. All the music, in its stark
simplicity, its hard, clear contours, its unsentimentality,
its non-pathetic sense of tragedy, is essentially Greek in
feeling.

Oedipus Rex is not without its disturbing factors.
The traditional elements seem to have been culled from
unnecessarily eclectic sources. One can discover the most
diverse backgrounds: Russian, Italian, German. There are
also occasional lapses into an earlier manner, as in the
shepherd's song, or moments such as the Oedipus solo
that follows, when the composer's consciousness of his
theory seems stronger than his musical invention.

The faults, however, cannot detract from the beauty of the music as a whole, nor from its value as an example of the new, impersonal approach to music. As such it is certain to exert a considerable influence on the younger generation. Other composers must interpret the new ideals according to their own lights. Later the neoclassic movement in music may be tempered by some compromise with romanticism.

London: 1931

THE INTERNATIONAL SOCIETY FOR CONTEMPORARY MUSIC gave its ninth annual festival at Oxford and London at the end of July. This group, which began so bravely at Salzburg in 1923, has recently been left in the embarrassing position of seeing the thing it had championed come to be taken for granted. Having won its cause, it no longer represents exclusively the most revolutionary tendencies in music, but exists rather to consecrate the glory of established reputations and to call to the attention of an international public the music of certain newer composers. Thus, it becomes increasingly important that the programs should be chosen with the utmost care. The festivals of the past few years have been severely criticized because this very point was their weakest. Fortunately this year's festival, held for the first time in England, helped somewhat to check the downward course.

The music given in London was more important than that given at Oxford, most of it being for large orchestra. Of this, the *Symphonic Music*, by Roman Palester, deserves first mention. The festival made a find in Palester, a young Pole of twenty-four whose name has hitherto been unknown, and who shows a strong flair for composition in spite of the obvious Stravinsky-Hindemith influences, influences that make his work characteristically modern. His piece had an exciting way about it, with sudden stops extremely telling in their effect, followed by crashing chords. The architectural form cannot be said to be faultless, yet at the same time it showed that the composer was well beyond the student's model-copy stage. Its peculiar structure gave it a disjointed quality that, though it prevented a welding of the three parts into a perfect whole, nevertheless gave it far more interest than if it had been less haphazard and merely more technically expert. Palester is a young composer who, in the usual phrase, "bears watching."

The orchestral piece that drew the most favorable general comment was Vladimir Vogel's *Two Studies for Orchestra*, which pleased both the public and the musicians. *Studies* is hardly the correct word. They seem much more to be two *"morceaux caractéristiques,"* of the type that in less pretentious forms were composed by minor Russians of the late nineteenth century. Musically considered, the two pieces are meaningless. They are academic concoctions and their emotional content is secondhand. The *Ritmica Funebre* stems from Mahler, not only in its emphatic bombast and its trite melodic contours, but also in its contrapuntal facture. The *Ritmica Scherzosa* is distinctly the better of the two, although it in turn fails to be original, and stems directly from Berlioz. This species of effective music, which sells modernity to the musical masses, will make the rounds of the orchestras for a time, and then be forgotten.

The problem child of the festival, eminently music one should not attempt to criticize after one hearing, was Webern's *Symphony for Small Orchestra*. It is to be regretted that the piece was presented in Queen's Hall, as its quality was decidedly too intimate for a large auditorium. There are certain things that can be said of Webern. His music has a wonderful poignancy, and a sensitivity that is related in some way to Debussy's; he can compress his emotional activity into a single moment, and he has absolute mastery over the means he employs. But there are certain other things that cannot yet be told: where, for example, is the point at which the exaggeration of a given quality renders a work anemic; to how much limitation of the emotional scale and of the musical means may a work be subjected—that is to say, when the idiom is more familiar, will one be able to differentiate among the various parts of what now appears to be of so even a tenor?

The only other work presenting any difficulties was Vladimir Dukelsky's *Second Symphony*, rather different from his songs and piano pieces. Those who considered Webern's work a problem would not generally have thought of this as one, since it is of an entirely different nature. Dukelsky has the making of a real style, obviously lyrical, and the difficulty consists in defining it. Certain aspects of his music relate him to Prokofieff: a fresh melodic gift, an aristocratic charm and grace, and an easy flair. The exact quality of the style, however, is not so easily grasped, in as much as it is less apparent, and the music in general possibly has fewer mannerisms than Prokofieff's. The conception of this symphony appeared to be related rather to voice forms than to symphonic music.

Played on the same program was Constant Lambert's *Music for Orchestra*. This work commanded particular attention as coming from a man of twenty-six who, with William Walton, is generally looked upon in England as the "white hope" of young British music. In spite of Lambert's youth one can safely characterize him a born academician. The whole process of his composition is diametrically opposed to the recherché and individualistic probings of Palester. It is good honest music built on clear-cut, honest themes that are interesting principally because of the way they avoid sounding like music by anyone else.

The *Three Symphonic Pieces,* by Juan José Castro, bore a certain resemblance to Palester's in that it was the surprisingly good work of an unknown composer, this time from Argentina. The pieces contained no facile South Americanisms. They displayed a fresh personality that seemed to have direct contact with the music created by it. Even the somewhat Wagnerian slow movement did nothing to mar the general effect of absolute sincerity.

A brilliant performance was given Vaughan Williams's *Benedicite* by the National Chorus and the British Broadcasting Corporation Orchestra. This had a certain bourgeois grandeur, a quality my British contemporaries find peculiarly English. Though dragged along involuntarily by the impetus of its flux, one was nevertheless unable to lose sight of the inherent banality of the materia musica. It is fairly safe to predict that Vaughan Williams will be the kind of local composer who stands for something great in the musical development of his own country but whose actual musical contribution cannot bear exportation. Besides, he is essentially not modern at all; at any rate, no more so than Rimsky-Korsakoff. This is of course no fault, but it means that Williams lives in a world that is no longer ours, a condition that results in music unrelated to life as we know it. His is the music of a gentleman-farmer, noble in inspiration, but dull.*

It is regrettable that Albert Roussel's *Psalm 80,* for chorus and orchestra, came so late in the two-and-a-half-

* Subsequent works, especially the composer's *Symphony No. 4,* give the lie to this statement.

hour program. It was practically impossible to hear it properly. Still, the impression remains that it was not Roussel of the first water; it lacked that acidulous quality, that sense of pleasant but painful effort that seems necessary for his best work. The *Psalm* was most impressive in the effect it gave of proportion and mass. Nevertheless, judgment should be suspended until the work is better known.

Of all the chamber music performed the *Sonata for Piano* by Roger Sessions was by far the most important. This is not a composition to be heard once and then forgotten. Here is a solid piece of work—few composers in any country possess the artistic conscience that such finished music implies. One must admire the mastery that enabled Sessions to build the satisfying proportions of the whole, the subtle transitions from movement to movement, the singing line of the introduction and slow movement. These will be clear to anyone who takes the trouble to study the published score. The *Sonata*, however, is not merely an example of perfected technique; it is music of character. Sessions adopts a "universal" style, a style without any of the earmarks of obvious nationalism, and within this "universality" he is able to express an individuality robust and direct, simple and tender, and of a special sensitivity. Peculiarly characteristic is a certain quiet melancholy one finds in the middle section of the slow movement, a melancholy neither sentimental nor depressing in effect, but lyrical and profound. To perceive this personality, the listener must have an intimate acquaintance with the music; no cursory examination will suffice. To know the work well is to have the firm conviction that Sessions has presented us with a cornerstone upon which to base an American music.

Not least in value was the opportunity the festival supplied to gain a more intimate contact with English musicians. It is perhaps not generally realized that they form a separate species, as distinct in character as the Russians, French, or Germans. There is a body of musical opinion in England of which we know nothing in America, a sense of standard that adds dignity to British musical life. Once again it was made clear that the furtherance of *rapprochement* among musicians of different countries is one of the most important services these annual festivals perform.

•

Berlin: 1932

THE ONLY RIVAL New York has as the principal center of interest in world musical affairs is Berlin. The fall season began auspiciously in that city—it carried off the two most important premières given anywhere. One was Stravinsky's *Concerto for Violin in D*, which, after its performance by the Berlin Radio Corporation, for which it was especially written, was immediately snatched up by London, Paris, Boston, Philadelphia, New York, etc. The other was Hindemith's latest opus and first essay in the field of oratorio, *Das Unaufhörliche*, which has not yet been heard outside Germany.

The Hindemith oratorio was awaited with more than ordinary curiosity. In the past few years Hindemith has given his admirers cause for misgivings. He was told so by one of them in a remarkable "Open Letter to Paul Hindemith," which appeared in a German periodical some time ago. The danger was clear: Hindemith's extraordinary musical facility was getting out of hand; he was writing music not because he had to but because he was able to. The new work would indicate how this still-young composer was to use his phenomenal gifts in the near future.

Das Unaufhörliche is a full-length oratorio, set for the usual combination of chorus, soloists, organ, and orchestra on a text by the contemporary German poet, Gottfried Benn. No exact English equivalent exists for *Das Unaufhörliche*; approximately it means that-indefinable-something-in-life-that-never-ends. The idea of the poem is to glorify in modern terms what Shaw has called the Life Force, and Bergson the *élan vital*, an idea that Benn himself admits is not new. He chose to clothe it with language that in its short sentence structure approaches that of the essayist, rather than with the florid arabesque of poetic imagination. Here was an opportunity for Hindemith, the man who had given new life to German music, the creator of so many pages that are vital and alive, to sing one great and overpowering Yea to the inexorable Fates that hold us all in thrall.

To our utmost astonishment he did no such thing. What we heard was undoubtedly Hindemith's sincerest reaction to the poem, but the mood he created was not very different from what Brahms or Mahler might have given us with the same text. Instead of the reaction of young blood to the age-old conception of Acceptance, we were presented with a work that was in every respect an oratorio, the dear old dead oratorio, with its sanctimonious and familiar stench.

It was this overwhelmingly conventional note that spoiled whatever merit the separate solos and choruses had. And they were not without merit—sometimes even deeply moving, as in one or two of the soprano solos that are of an almost French charm and grace, or certain choruses (such as the final one) that are planned on a monumental scale and are very telling in effect. But as a whole the work is monotonous and lacks that sense of elation, that catharsis, that every good work of art should give us.

3. THE COMPOSERS
OF SOUTH AMERICA: 1941*

ONE AFTERNOON IN 1923 I was introduced to a short and dynamic individual at the Paris apartment of my composition teacher, Nadia Boulanger. Someone told me that this gentleman with the dark complexion and the fiery eyes was a composer from Brazil by the name of Heitor Villa-Lobos. This was the first inkling I had that there might be such a thing as Latin American music. Up to that time we all naturally assumed that the exciting new music would come from Europe. A few daring spirits had the temerity to hope that the United States might someday contribute to the stream of world composition. But practically nobody had given a thought to South America as a possible source for fresh musical experience.

My second contact with Latin American composi-

* Caution: This article was composed in 1941. Statements no longer true are amended or ameliorated in footnotes.

tion was made in Greenwich Village. In a tiny one-room apartment where he lived around 1927, Carlos Chávez played for me his Mexican ballet *The Four Suns*. I was enthusiastic about what I heard, and this time the concept of a Latin American music really stuck.

The idea has since been gaining hold everywhere. Recently world conditions (and political expediency) have provided an unexpected impetus to our musical relations with neighboring American countries. By now, of course, both Villa-Lobos and Chávez are familiar figures in the musical world. And my own interest broadened considerably, after a first, tentative visit to Mexico in 1932, and in 1941 a musical tour through nine different countries of the Southern Hemisphere.

I doubt whether anyone in Peru or Ecuador had ever before seen an American symphonic composer in the flesh. To get quite so far afield, you have to be possessed, as I am, of a kind of musical wanderlust. Too many people, when it comes to music, are inveterate stay-at-homes. They apparently feel uncomfortable except when they are in the presence of accredited genius. They prefer to wander down well-worn paths, clearly marked: "This Way to a Masterpiece." But it has been my experience that those who really love music have a consuming passion to become familiar with its every manifestation. Without doubt, one of the newest of those manifestations is Latin American music, and, fortunately for music listeners, they have had in recent years many more opportunities to get acquainted with it.

Most musical people want to know whether there are any interesting composers in the southern part of our hemisphere. They are willing to take yes or no for an answer and let it go at that. For the musician who has been visiting the composers in South America, as I have been, the answer is not so simple. I examined the work of about sixty-five composers and didn't find a Bach or Beethoven among them. But I did find an increasing body of music, many well-trained composers, a few real personalities, and great promise for the future. Enough to make apparent the value for both North and South America of closer, more permanent musical ties, beyond any question of political expediency.

To see the field of composition as it actually is down there, we should of course stop thinking in terms of "The South American Composer." No such person exists. South America, as we are often told but never seem fully to comprehend, is a collection of separate countries, each with independent traditions. Their musical developments are various and there is little or no musical contact between them. Brazilian, Colombian, Peruvian composers are just as different from each other as are Dutch, Hungarian, or Yugoslav composers. European music covers a lot of territory, and so also does South American.

Certain generalizations are possible, however. The countries that have developed most quickly are those with the richest folklore. But whether folklorism is strong or not, the influence of the modern French school is predominant everywhere in South America. This is true of all the arts, but particularly of music. A few of the more sophisticated composers are thoroughly familiar with early Stravinsky and are at times influenced by what they know. As for Schönberg or Hindemith, their names are known and their music admired, but they have as yet left very few traces.* The Latin strain in South American art is a strong one, and it will undoubtedly continue to be so.

All contemporary composers in South America produce works under serious handicaps. Only five or six first-rate orchestras function on the entire continent. Comparatively few performances of new works are given by these orchestras, and the same holds true for the local radio stations. Shorter pieces have been published from time to time, but publishers are entirely lacking for long and serious works. Many composers labor in isolation, with little hope of reaching any live audience. The wonder is that, despite these conditions, so many new works are written each year.

The degree of musical progress differs in each country. In some the composers are more personalized, in others musical organization is better, in still others it is the concert activity that is richest. In general, the countries with the deepest Indian strain seem to promise most for the future. The best way to look at South American

* These statements are no longer true in 1960. The Schönberg school has had considerable influence, and the Debussy-Ravel aesthetic has been replaced by a strong interest in United States composers of various tendencies.

composition is to approach it, country by country, starting with those known as the ABC group, where most musical activity is centered.

ARGENTINA

There has been a tendency, it seems to me, to underestimate the music written by Argentina's composers. As yet one cannot honestly speak of an Argentine school, since a strikingly indigenous profile is lacking. Nevertheless, as a whole, composers of Argentina are more cultivated and more professionally prepared than any similar group to be found in Latin America. Moreover, musical life in Buenos Aires is really cosmopolitan in scope—all the finest artists are heard and a considerable amount of unfamiliar music is performed each season.

Contemporary musical effort suffers considerably because of a small group of conservative musicians who completely control government musical policy. That is very serious in a country where so much activity is subsidized through official channels. Much harm has also been done by a superstition current in polite musical circles that only compositions inspired by Argentine folklore can possibly be any good. The composer who dares to ignore that unwritten fiat is likely to see his works go unperformed.

Most of the new music heard in Buenos Aires is presented in concerts of the Grupo Renovación or La

Nueva Música, two modern-music societies comparable to our own League of Composers. The older is the Grupo Renovación, whose principal composer members are Jacobo Ficher, Honorio Siccardi, Luis Gianneo, and José María Castro. Of these Castro seems to me to possess the strongest creative instinct. (It should be explained that José María is the eldest of four brothers, all musicians, of whom Juan José is the well-known composer-conductor recently active in this country.) José María's music, practically unknown here, fits easily into one of two categories: it is either neoclassic of the bright and happy kind—a rare phenomenon in South America—or it is neoromantic with a bitter-sweet flavor entirely personal to the composer. In either case the music he writes is entirely without affectation—refreshingly simple and direct, reflecting the impression he makes as a human being. Castro ought to be much better known, not only in the United States, but also in his own country.

La Nueva Música, the second of these organizations, is headed by the Argentine composer Juan Carlos Paz. Paz has a broader acquaintance with the literature of modern music than any other musician I met in South America. He is an indefatigable worker—serious, learned, solitary, and something of a martyr to the "cause." Paz is the only mature composer in South America who has attached himself to the Schönberg twelve-tone line. It is characteristic that there is no faintest suggestion of caterwauling in Paz's twelve-tone system. It is as cool and detached and precise as any diagram, the kind of music that is always a pleasure to look at, if not always a pleasure to hear. What he lacks most as a composer is the real lyric urge; much of his work takes on a grayish pallor that in the end is tiring. Technically it is first class, but artistically it is distinguished rather than exciting.

All groups are agreed, however, that the white hope of Argentine music is young Alberto Ginastera. Ginastera has a natural flair for writing brilliantly effective, sure-fire music of the French-Spanish persuasion. Sometimes it acquires an increased charm through a well-placed use of local melodic phraseology. He also possesses an unusual knack for bright-sounding orchestrations. Later Ginastera may become more ambitious and learn to look inside himself for deeper sources. But already no report of music in Argentina is complete without mention of his name.

BRAZIL

The name of Heitor Villa-Lobos dominates all talk of musical composition in Brazil. Villa-Lobos is, of course, the dominating figure, not only in Brazil, but on the whole South American Continent. Still, this fact should not obscure the existence of other worthy men in his own country. Brazil, like Mexico, boasts a full-blooded school distinguishable from the European or any other model. This comparatively recent emergence is to be attributed to the fact that almost without exception Brazilian composers have frankly addressed themselves to their folklore, which is unusually rich, being based on four different sources—Negro, Indian, Portuguese, and even Spanish. Combine this with the sharply defined features of the Brazilian temperament, which is uninhibited, abundant, non-critical, romantic, and you get a music with more "face" than that of any other Latin-American nation.

But the blanket use of folk material carries with it certain dangers. In Brazil it narrows the field of action, for most composers confine themselves to the languorously sentimental or the wildly orgiastic mood, with very little between. Moreover, it encourages a type of romanticism that gives much of their music an old-fashioned touch—as if the essence had all been stated before, though not with the particular Brazilian twist. In this respect Mexican composers are more fortunate. The Mexican temperament is far more disciplined and therefore closer by nature to the generally sober line of new music.

Aside from its exclusive folklore bias Brazilian music suffers at present from a lack of what is called musical *ambiente*. The *ambiente*, or atmosphere, is definitely provincial, lacking stimulus for the wide-awake composer who wishes to keep abreast of the times. As a result, surprisingly few long or elaborate works are composed. Some ballets and a few operas have been written, but the balance sheet is weak as regards orchestral scores. On the other hand, literally hundreds of attractive songs and piano pieces have appeared in recent years, many of them have been published, and some few have even begun to find their way on American concert programs. That is where one hears the distinctive Brazilian note most easily —the sinuous melodies, the Negroid background rhythms, the peppery repeated notes, and the peculiar brand of nostalgia they called *saudade*.

For Brazilian art in general it is hard to find a more representative figure than Villa-Lobos, yet anyone evaluating his work takes on a heavy job. He has written hundreds of pieces in every cateogry. As I see it, the Villa-Lobos music has one outstanding quality—its abundance. That is its primary virtue. It is also at times enormously picturesque, free of musical prejudices, full of rhythmic vitality, sometimes cheap and vulgar with an overdose of figuration formulas—and sometimes astonishingly original. It has a way of being most effective on first hearing. Structurally the pieces are often loosely thrown together, making the impression of an inextricable mélange of authentic Brazilian atmosphere plus a full quota of modern French compositional processes. At his finest Villa-Lobos is a kind of zestful Brazilian Falla. His worst may be straight café concert music. He is always an absorbing composer because of his extraordinarily instinctive gift, which makes each composition unpredictable, full of surprises.

Some of the attention lavished on the work of Villa-Lobos could profitably be diverted to the music of Francisco Mignone, Camargo Guarnieri, or Lorenzo Fernandez.

Camargo Guarnieri, who is now about thirty-five, is

in my opinion the most exciting "unknown" talent in South America. His not inconsiderable body of works should be far better known than they are. Guarnieri is a real composer. He has everything it takes—a personality of his own, a finished technic, and a fecund imagination. His gift is more orderly than that of Villa-Lobos, though none-theless Brazilian. Like other Brazilians, he has the typical abundance, the typical romantic leanings (sometimes, surprisingly enough, in the direction of Ernest Bloch), and the usual rhythmic intricacies. The thing I like best about his music is its healthy emotional expression—it is the honest statement of how one man feels. There is, on the other hand, nothing particularly original about his music in any one department. He knows how to shape a form, how to orchestrate well, how to lead a bass line effectively. The thing that attracts one most in Guarnieri's music is its warmth and imagination, which are touched by a sensibility that is profoundly Brazilian. At its finest his is the fresh and racy music of a "new" continent.

CHILE

The fact that Chile is on the west coast of South America has made a great deal of difference in its musical history. It has lived a comparatively isolated musical life, maintaining only superficial relations with other South American countries. As a result, the capital city, Santiago, has developed a remarkably self-reliant and well-integrated

THE COMPOSERS OF SOUTH AMERICA: 1941

musical existence, in which the composers have taken a leading role. So far as musical organization goes, Chile is far in advance of the other Latin American countries. Most interesting musical events take place under the aegis of the faculty of fine arts of the University of Chile. Since the university is an autonomous body, subsidized by law but under no governmental control, the dean of the faculty is in an excellent position to carry on important cultural work in music. For example, the Orquesta Sinfónica de Chile is managed by the Fine Arts Department, which has allotted all the administrative posts to composers. The conductor is a native Chilean, the gifted Armando Carvajal. Obviously things are done differently here. Most of the setup is due to the efforts of the present Dean, Dr. Domingo Santa Cruz, a very energetic and competent musician.*

So far as composition goes, one continues to see the group tendency strongly in evidence—this time, however, with less good results. Chilean music lacks outside air. Forming only a small circle (though surprisingly numerous in relation to the size of Santiago), Chilean composers influence each other too much. Their music is not as fresh as it might be. There is a definite overstressing of the nostalgic note—a kind of Ravel-like nostalgia, thickened by complex chromatic chords that seem more complex than is absolutely necessary. I miss the bold and affirmative note that one expects in the music of a newly

* Dr. Santa Cruz, now retired from his post, has seen his work continued by his former pupils and colleagues.

developing country. I hasten to add, however, that the composers with whom I spoke seemed well aware of these limitations and intent upon developing the national musical creativity along broader lines.

The outstanding composer is, without doubt, Domingo Santa Cruz. His technic is extremely solid, far in advance of most composers on the West Coast. But, like our own Roger Sessions, Santa Cruz is more the philosopher-composer than the composer pure and simple. This gives his music, particularly the recent examples, a scholarly look that makes one respect rather than love it. Still, the recent *Five Short Pieces for String Orchestra* has warmth within the neoclassic frame that inspires renewed interest in the working of this inquisitive mind.

Humberto Allende, now a man of about sixty, is one of South America's most sensitive composers. It is easy to enjoy the best of his music, but it undoubtedly lacks variety. His most famous composition, the twelve *Tonadas* for piano, is sad and poetic. But the sadness and poetry are real, underneath the Parisian veneer, vintage 1923. He has taught many of the younger men and is looked upon with much affection by his confreres.

Carlos Isamitt is both painter and composer. His musical works may be divided briefly into those based on Araucanian Indian melodies, and those without any folk material. Personally I much prefer the Araucanian works. The others suffer badly from a type of harmony that is far too peculiar to be real. Isamitt's music would improve if he were able to inject into his work some of the quiet charm of his personality.

The younger generation is best represented by René Amengual and Alfonso Letelier, both in their early thirties. Letelier has the more spontaneity, but Amengual has more technic. What they both need is a larger experience of the whole field of modern music.*

OTHER COUNTRIES

Uruguay has an active musical life though it is confined almost entirely to the capital city of Montevideo. Unfortunately it has failed to exploit its composers, of whom there are very few. But one of the most impressive new talents in all South America is a Uruguayan, Hector Tosar, a quiet, nervous youth of eighteen who is studying law and music simultaneously. He has a vivid imagination, dash, and *élan*; his music reminds me a little of Shostakovich. It is still student work, naturally, but very promising.

In Colombia, Peru, and Ecuador musical composition is still in its infancy. (This is said to be even more true of Paraguay, Bolivia, and Venezuela,** a report I was

* Humberto Allende died in 1959 and René Amengual in 1954. The outstanding representative of the younger generation at the present time is the gifted Juan Orrego-Salas.

** Two important festivals of Latin American orchestral music took place in Venezuela in the fifties. Antonio Esteves emerged as a Venezuelan composer of consequence.

not able to verify by personal observation.) Several factors account for this—the lack of any rigorous training for composers, a *dolce far niente* attitude on the part of the students, and a generally low ebb of musical activity. The only composers whose work is worth serious consideration, Guillermo Uribe Holguín in Colombia and André Sas in Peru, are European-trained.

Sas is a naturalized Peruvian who was born in Belgium but has lived in Lima for almost twenty years. He has written mostly songs, piano or violin pieces, tastefully done in the Gallic manner. He claims to be too busy with his teaching to engage in longer works for orchestra. Many of his pieces are based on Inca material, but this is no more than a detail since in spirit Sas can be thought of only as European. While in Lima I was fortunate in hearing a group of native performers called the Conjunto Vivanco, who produced a fascinating music on homemade harps, violins, flutes, rattles and ram's-horns. Someday a Peruvian composer will be able to re-create the music I heard in terms of a symphonic combination, in the way that Chávez has done for Mexican native music.

Uribe Holguín has been Colombia's outstanding musician for a good many years. At sixty he has a long list of works to his credit, only a very few of which I was able to examine. These seemed definitely on the French side, as would be natural in a man who trained in Paris under D'Indy. They did not, however, give the impression of being carefully done, though the musical quality was pleasant enough.

A musical roundup of South American composers would not normally include Cuba, but there is no doubt that culturally and musically Cuba belongs with the Latin American countries. Serious music in Cuba suffered a setback in the death of its two leading men—Amadeo Roldán in 1939 and Alejandro Caturla in 1940. The only composer of importance now writing works there in the larger forms is José Ardévol, a naturalized Spaniard of thirty, who has taken Roldán's place as the teacher of most of Havana's young composers. He is a very intelligent musician and a gifted artist. His recent works stem directly from the neoclassic aesthetic, giving them at times a too great similarity of style and emotional content. Still, they are well worth exportation, and should be heard in this country.

Cuba has a folk music comparable in interest to that of Brazil. No one seems to be carrying on the tradition set by Roldán and Caturla of using that material as a basis for serious composition.* Gilberto Valdés, who composes *música típica* for his radio orchestra, comes closest to fitting into this category. With more training and greater discipline he might even become the Gershwin of Cuban music.

Today one may wonder why we have been so little conscious of the music of South America. But from now on, whatever other result the world crisis may bring, it is a safe bet that musical relations with our southern neighbors will be different.

* This remains largely true, even of the work of Julián Orbón, Cuba's most gifted composer of the new generation.

SECTION THREE

The Reviewing Stand

Darius Milhaud (1947)

I HAVE OFTEN WONDERED what the "big"
public thinks about the music of Darius Milhaud. If they
like it, what is it they warm up to, and if they dislike it,
what puts them off? In spite of the large quantities of it
available on radio and in concert there seems to be a curious lack of vocal enthusiasm in regard to Milhaud's music.
More recondite composers like Schönberg or Bartók have
their devoted followers, while Mahler and Sibelius are
listened to rapturously by fervent adherents. Milhaud, apparently, is headed for a different fate. He once wrote: "I
have no esthetic rules, or philosophy, or theories. I love to
write music. I always do it with pleasure, otherwise I just
do not write it." You can't hope to arouse a following on
the basis of any plain statement like that.

Nevertheless it seems to me fairly obvious that since

Ravel's death France has given us no composer more important than Darius Milhaud.

I became a Milhaud fan back in the early twenties, when the composer was considered the *enfant terrible* of French music. In those days we were struck by the abundance and many-sidedness of his talent, his forthrightness and fearlessness, his humor, his humanity, the contrasts of tenderness and violence, and his markedly personal style. Most striking of all in an age when the new music was being accused of having no melody was the singing quality of Milhaud's music. After nearly thirty years I continue to marvel at Milhaud's apparently inexhaustible productive capacity, at his stylistic consistency, at the sheer creative strength that the body of his work represents. Those who persist in describing modern music as decadent and desiccated will get little comfort from this man's music.

Milhaud's finest work will probably be found in the operatic field. But it is good to have these two recently recorded examples of his orchestral literature. The *Symphony No. 1* is particularly welcome because it is a comparatively new opus (1939) that has had few hearings. It was composed on commission from the Chicago Symphony as part of the celebration of that orchestra's fiftieth anniversary, and was first heard in Chicago under the composer's baton. In category it belongs with the less accessible of his works. By which I mean you will have to hear this score more than once before you can hope to uncover its own special secret.

Like Brahms, Milhaud waited until he was in his middle forties before embarking on the writing of a symphony. But that is about the only similarity one will find. In order to properly evaluate this *Symphony No. 1* it will be necessary to have no preconceived notions of what a proper symphony is like. The symphony as a form is confused in our minds with what the nineteenth century thought it ought to be. True, Milhaud's symphony has the usual four movements (of a duration somewhat briefer than usual) but the familiar hortatory manner is lacking. It is a songful symphony, though not cheerfully songful like the "Italian" of Mendelssohn. The first movement, for example, has long-lined melodies, but they are accompanied by darkly tinted and unhappy-sounding harmonies. Milhaud has a particular aptitude for suggesting the complexities of modern life, even at times embroiling himself in analogous musical complexities. The second movement of this symphony is a case in point. It presents the listener with a changeful panorama and an intricate fabric, a little frightening in its noisiness. It would be easy to lose one's bearing here, but if we listen carefully for the principal melodic strand, it will lead us through the movement like a thread through a labyrinth.

Perhaps the most impressive movement of the entire symphony is the third—the slow movement. The opening chords in quiet brass are steeped in Milhaud's personal idiom—producing a drugged and nostalgic effect. Seriousness of tone and warmth of expression are the keynote. A curious mixture of Gallic exoticisms and "blues" atmosphere combine to create the typical Milhaud *ambiance*. He snaps us out of it, so to speak, in a finale that is scherzo-like by nature, with square-cut themes in 6/8 rhythm. There is a surprisingly close affinity with Scottish folk melody and nasal bagpipe sonorities. As in the second movement there are strong contrasts of light and shade, raucous brass, and a rather complicated structural frame. Considered as a whole, this is not an easy work to assimilate. But I strongly suspect that it will repay repeated hearings. The performance by the Columbia Symphony Orchestra under the composer's direction appears to be well balanced and is certainly authoritative.

On the final side of the fourth record is the recording of a short orchestral elegy entitled "In Memoriam," representative of the composer's most sober style.

For those who may have missed it when it was released some months ago, there is an excellent account of a *Symphonic Suite*—vintage of 1919—culled from the music Milhaud composed for Paul Claudel's satirical drama *Protée*. The first performance of the suite in Paris in 1920 resulted in a near-riot. The public was quite convinced that the composer was mad. It's amusing to listen to this same music in 1948, played by Pierre Monteux and the San Francisco Symphony. Obviously, it is the music of a brash young man, not at all perturbed at the idea of shocking his audience. My guess would be that it was the clashing polytonal harmonies that were largely responsible for the upsetting effect the music had on its first listeners.

The newness of effect has worn off, but not the essential freshness of the music. My favorite among the five movements is the "Nocturne," a poetic fancy that never fails to move me. Delightful is the word for Proteus.

Benjamin Britten (1947)

THE INTERESTING THING about Benjamin Britten's new opera, *The Rape of Lucretia,* is the impression one gets that it is better than his opera *Peter Grimes.* This is significant in view of the fact that Britten is still in his early thirties, that he is now engaged on another opera, and that he is likely to compose several more. *Grimes* was an opera in the usual sense; *Lucretia* is a chamber opera, designed for eight singers and twelve instrumentalists. It is part of a trilogy of chamber operas planned by the composer for the repertory needs of a specific company of singers and players.

Britten has been, since the start of his career, a boy wonder. Something of the aura of the boy wonder still hangs about him. I know of no other composer alive today who writes music with such phenomenal flair. Other composers write with facility, but Britten's facility is breath-taking. He combines an absolutely solid technical equipment with a reckless freedom in handling the more complex compositional textures. The whole thing is carried off with an abandon and verve that are irresistible. The resultant music may not always be of the best quality, but it is certainly of a unique quality—for there is no one in contemporary music who is remotely like him.

The operatic form provides plenty of elbowroom for Britten's special "flair." *Grimes* and *Lucretia*, despite their differences, are shaped out of a similar mold. Britten's operas show every sign of being carefully planned from first word to final note. Nothing is improvised, nothing left to chance. His planning starts with the libretto, in this case the work of Ronald Duncan, based on an original French play by André Obey. Operatic treatment, as Britten understands it, breaks up into three different types: the usual recitative to move the plot ahead; a more florid, accompanied recitative for dramatic pointing up; the fully developed aria, duo, septet, etc., for carrying the emotional burden. This comparatively simple formula is rigorously applied, and makes for coherent plotting of the entire work. The danger for the future lies in the possibility of an overdose of planning.

Probably the most striking single factor in his operatic writing is the richness, variety, breadth, and sweep of his melodic lines. The elements that make up the line are not always original. But even when they are eclectic to a disturbing degree it is the power behind the musical impulse that puts them over. This same richness of melodic invention, when applied to choral writing, produces brilliant results. Unlike the American operas of Blitzstein and Virgil Thomson, Britten's world does not rely upon the speech rhythms and inflections to give his melodic line naturalness. Quite the contrary. Britten is not primarily interested in naturalness, and is even not averse to deliberate distortions of prosodic treatment if he can achieve greater expressivity and expansiveness thereby.

A word must be added about the amazing variety of effects he is able to extract from his twelve instrumentalists. When one considers that two hours of opera are accompanied by a dozen players one marvels at the subtlety and imagination and ingenuity of the orchestration.

A fully rounded judgment of *The Rape of Lucretia* should await stage presentation in our country.* I have serious reservations as to the validity of certain scenes in the libretto. The piano-vocal score (in an excellent version by Henry Boys) taken by itself, however, would seem to me to repay closest study on the part of anyone interested in contemporary opera.

* First presented in Chicago, June 1947.

Stefan Wolpe (1948)

IN THE WELTER of musical activity in America the publication of two more songs would seem to make little difference one way or another. But these songs (*Two Songs for Alto and Piano* from the *Song of Songs*) are exceptional. They draw attention to the work of Stefan Wolpe, one of the most remarkable of living composers. And they draw attention also to the venturesome Hargail Music Press, to whom we are indebted for more than one unlikely publication.

America doesn't seem to know what to do with strong talents like Wolpe. If his music were less grimly serious, less stark, less uncompromising, it would undoubtedly fare better in the musical market place. Although Wolpe has been composing and teaching among us for the past decade (he arrived here from Germany via Palestine about 1939), only a small group of professionals and pupils have come to know his value. To me Wolpe's music is strikingly original, with a kind of fiery inner logic that makes for fascinated listening. Some pounding natural force brings it forth and gives it reality. It is a sad commentary on the state of our musical house that this man must create in comparative isolation. Wolpe is definitely someone to be discovered.

These two compositions for alto and piano, with text from the *Song of Songs*, are part of a larger series of Palestinian songs. Wolpe has put the essence of himself in these songs in something of the same way that *Das Marienleben* contains in microcosm the essence of Hindemith. They are intensely alive, deeply Jewish, and very personal. The first of the two alto songs is especially characteristic: the curiously restless rhythmic structure, the bareness and severity of the two-part piano accompaniment, the fresh flavorsome quality of the folklike melodic line. By comparison, the second song is less arresting, though it is by ordinary standards nobly expressive. Both songs demand superior interpreters. They make one keenly anticipate the publication of the remainder of Wolpe's Palestinian songs.

Leon Kirchner (1950)

COMPOSED IN 1947, this *Duo for Violin and Piano*
is the first published composition of Leon Kirchner, a
comparative newcomer to the American musical scene. I
doubt whether a more important young American composer has come along since the advent of Harold Shapero
several years back. Recent New York performances of
Kirchner's *Duo,* his *Piano Sonata,* and most recently his
String Quartet No. 1 were accorded a unanimity of enthusiasm that is rare in the case of a hitherto-unknown
name. It is all the more unusual since his music is not by
any means of the easily assimilable kind, belonging as it
does to the Bartók-Berg axis of contemporary music.

Kirchner is a Brooklynite who pursued his musical
studies in California, where he was a student of Roger
Sessions. (He also did some work on the West Coast with
Bloch and Schönberg.) In considering the teachers he
sought out, and the clearly chromatic propensities of his
own music, it is rather surprising that Kirchner has not

been won over to adopting the twelve-tone system *in toto*. The fact that he has not is indicative of an independent mind, an independence that shows itself in other aspects of his music.

Studying this first available work of Kirchner's, I am struck by how little the written notes convey the strong impression made by a live performance of the *Duo*. It is well to keep this in mind—the potential effect of these notes when performed in the concert hall; otherwise I am afraid that the purchaser may be a trifle disappointed. For a measure-by-measure examination of the *Duo* will disclose nothing remarkable in the way of melodic invention or rhythmic novelty. Nor is there anything remarkable about Kirchner's harmonic vocabulary, which reflects current practice in advanced creative circles.

And yet, undeniably, when sounded in actual performance, the notes themselves cast a spell. What is the explanation? I am not sure that I know. But what I do know is that the impression carried away from a Kirchner performance is one of having made contact, not merely with a composer, but with a highly sentient human being; of a man who creates his music out of an awareness of the special climate of today's unsettled world. Kirchner's best pages prove that he reacts strongly to that world; they are charged with an emotional impact and explosive power that are almost frightening in intensity. Whatever else may be said, this is music that most certainly is "felt." No wonder his listeners have been convinced.

In studying the *Duo* one inevitably thinks of Bartók,

since there is obviously a similarity of aesthetic approach in both composers. But in the case of the Hungarian master the basic emotional turmoil, the bitterness and pessimism, is tempered by a meticulous workmanship, almost schoolmasterish in its manipulation of musical materials. Bartók's is a controlled violence, in which the element of control is a mitigating circumstance. But with Kirchner, although he works with analogous material, we get the impression of a creative urge so vital as to burst all bonds of ordinary control. It is this out-of-control quality that gives any one of his works enormous excitement. To date it would seem to me that that is his principal claim to originality: the daringly free structural organization of his compositions. Certain it is that the *Duo*, cast in a one-movement form, will never make the analysis boys happy. One literally never knows what is likely to happen next, and sometimes the composer seems no more sure than ourselves. But I respect his willingness to take such chances, for the future is sure to require a more experimental attitude toward formal problems on the part of composers.

The road ahead will not be easy for a composer of Kirchner's gifts and pretensions. All the more reason why we shall watch with special concern what the next work will bring.

William Schuman (1951)

A COMPOSITION LIKE the *String Quartet No. 4* makes one understand why Schuman is generally ranked among the top men in American music. Even a single hearing made it evident that this is one of Schuman's most mature works. A second hearing confirmed the impression. This is music written with true urgency: compact in form, ingenious in its instrumental technique, quite experimental as to harmony. In some ways it is typical of the composer, in others it seems to be composed from a new premise.

It is the way in which it is different that interests me most. I cannot remember another work of Schuman that strikes so somber a note. The old full-throated, free-singing eloquence, so characteristic of some of his best pages, is little in evidence. Instead a more tentative expressivity has taken over; a darker, more forbidding tone that seems far different from the basically optimistic—sometimes boyishly optimistic—tone of his earlier music.

Much of this darker texture comes from the harmonic fabric, which is less tonally defined than in former works by this composer, and teeters on the edge of the atonal. I may be wrong, but it seems to me that I detect, if not an influence, then a stimulus to the composer's thinking from contact with the music of Roger Sessions. At any rate no other work of Schuman's is so consistently dissonant in chordal structure. At times, especially in the third movement, the composer employs a device he has used only in his latest works; it is based largely on simultaneously sounded major and minor intervals, mostly thirds and sixths. The final measures of this slow movement are a good example of this procedure, with its major-minor intervals that produce chords of a bitter-sweet expressiveness, and make for a considerable unity of style. It is the wavering between the diatonic and chromatic implications of chords such as these, alternatively suggestive of strain and then relaxed tension, that gives the work its character. Not all the harmonic textures of the other movements are equally convincing: in a strained and "painful" harmonic complex it isn't likely that each measure will come out as happily, so to speak, as one would like. (The same might be said of certain Schönberg pieces.) But it is the over-all experimental attitude that augurs well for the future; the sense one has that a new (for Schuman) expressive content rendered the old formulas inadequate, leading him in a direction that is likely to enrich his style.

Schuman's masterful handling of instrumental color and rhythmic ingenuity is again demonstrated in the new quartet. The second and final movements of the work contain those curiously Schumanesque rhythms, so skittish and personal, so utterly free and inventive. As usual with Schuman, these rhythms are all innocently fitted into regular metric divisions, but they are devilish to perform nonetheless, because the true rhythmic impulse makes a mockery of the bar-line. Schuman uses the bar-line as a railing, to prevent his performers—and perhaps himself also—from toppling over into rhythmic chaos. One holds one's breath as these rhythms bound along—sometimes easily, sometimes a little awkwardly (is that the players' fault?)—skipping and leaping about, losing a quarter here and gaining a triplet there, with sudden pauses of unpredictable length, the whole thing carried off with exhilarating effect. There is nothing quite like these rhythms in American music, or any other music for that matter.

His instrumental writing is idiomatic, and at the same time original. Schuman isn't afraid to take chances with his four strings, and for the most part his daring is justified by the dash and brilliance of the result. I am thinking of the section of four-part pizzicato chords, strummed *fortississimo* by each of the performers in the last movement; or the quiet opening double-stopped chords of the slow movement, curiously suggestive of a kind of organ-string tone. Schuman is conscious of his players at every instant; he knows how to combine sonorities for the strings that would sound ugly on the piano or in a brass ensemble, combinations that give bite and color to a medium that can easily become oversensitized, and even cloying.

Technically the greatest advance is in the composer's handling of the formal problem in this work. Schuman has always had a strong structural sense, but he has not always succeeded in filling out his forms with music all the way. By that I mean one sensed the effort it cost the composer to round out a long form—the dangerous area being the long pull to the climax before turning the corner to the restatement of the opening material. More than once a forced and laborious climb spoiled the natural ease of an opening section. This quartet has no such blemish. The first and last movements are compactly shaped; the second movement and especially the third are more extensively developed, yet fully realized. The whole leaves an impression of a varied and well-balanced content.

In retrospect it is clear that this work will not gain Schuman new adherents among the lay public. Even a cultivated audience will be put off by a certain hermetic quality at its core. But it is just this hermetic quality— this somewhat forbidding and recalcitrant aspect—that presages an enlargement of the capacities of the William Schuman we already know.

Virgil Thomson's Musical State (1939)

VIRGIL THOMSON has written the most original book on music that America has produced. *The State of Music* is the wittiest, the most provocative, the best written, the least conventional book on matters musical I have ever seen (always excepting Berlioz). If you want to have fun, watch how people react to this book. It will undoubtedly be taken too solemnly by some, not solemnly enough by others. It will make many readers hopping mad. It will simply delight others. It will be quoted and discussed everywhere. In other words, it is the book that every reader of *Modern Music* would expect Virgil Thomson to write—a book that only he could have written.

Composers especially can profit by reading it. *The State of Music* is primarily a discussion of their own profession. There is very little about good and bad composers, good and bad music. Thomson is positively squeamish about judging other men's music. Instead he describes the composer's general situation in the Musical State and in the world at large. For once the composer is treated as a human being, with not merely a craftsman's interest, but also economic, political, and social interests. One can violently disagree with àny number of Thomson's conclusions on these matters, but the composer *qua* composer emerges from these pages as a personage, *un homme*.

Thomson has an almost medieval sense of the composer's professional community of interests—both financial and artistic. He is strongly for a composer's united front *vis-à-vis* the home government (whatever form it may take—democratic or authoritarian), the music employers (whether they be publishers, patronesses, or radio stations), and the music consumers. (What music-lovers are to you are just plain customers to him.) Professional solidarity is about the only thing preached in this book.

The composer, according to Thomson, is a miniature capitalist, with "vested interests" in his compositions. This makes him different from the musical executant, who, being paid a wage on an hourly basis, is properly organized in trade-unions, affiliated with other trade-unions. The composer, like the doctor, the lawyer, or the literary man, is more properly organized in guilds or alliances. The present setup, in which composers and publishers band together for the collection of performing rights, is less desirable than a possible future alliance between the composers and their executants. As far as I know Thomson is the first composer among us who has ever

considered these things. Everyone else has been so busy
upholding artistic ideals that they have completely lost
sight of the composer's professional status as such.

Money is a word that doesn't frighten Thomson. *Au
contraire*, he likes it. It explains a great many otherwise
inexplicable things. Musical style, for instance. Tell
Thomson how you make your money and he will tell you
what your musical style is likely to be. In the highly diverting chapter on "Why Composers Write How" (the
economic determinism of musical style), composers'
possible income sources are tabulated with devastating
completeness. Heaven help you if you live off the "appreciation racket." A composer, says V.T., can sink no
lower. On the other hand, he exudes a warm glow when
writing about that *rara avis*—the composer who can support himself exclusively from collections of royalties on
the sale or performance of his music. "Royalties and per-
forming-rights fees are to any composer a sweetly solemn
thought" is the way he puts it. It's a chapter with a great
deal of real observation in it, despite an overdose of continuous generalizations.

The composer as a political animal is another of
Thomson's preoccupations. It keeps cropping up on
every other page. If I understand him correctly, Thomson
has no quarrel with the individual composer who dabbles
in politics. He thinks that said composer might be better
employed working at his music at home, but still, there
is no great harm in it. What he will not have, however, is
that the composers' organization be involved in the affairs

of any particular political party, rightist, leftist, or liberal. He firmly maintains that the proper province of the composers' organization is the setting of *musical* policies. "We must demand . . . from any governing agency of whatever kind in any possible state, both economic security for our members and the musical direction of all enterprises of whatever nature where music is employed." I strongly suspect an oversimplification here. But whatever its value as a program for the future, it makes sense here and now in America, where composers have no control over musical affairs, let alone political ones.

Composers are not Thomson's sole concern in the State of Music. There are very amusing sketches of the artists in neighboring states—the painters, the poets, the architects, the actors, the photographers. The dancers, poor dears, rate only one sentence. They are "autoerotic and lack conversation."

Under the pretext of telling "How to Write a Piece" there are excellent analyses of the considerable problems involved in writing music for the screen, the stage, the ballet, and the opera. Thomson knows whereof he speaks, having written successfully in all these forms himself. He has sound advice to give, worth the attention of any composer. His handling of concert music is touched by a certain amount of personal acrimony. "It is a very intense little affair," he says. The shortcomings of the concert field are gone over once again, without adding very much to an already-sore subject.

But Thomson's really big guns are reserved for that

special field of the concert world known as "modern music." He sees an International Modern Music Ring, (something like Father Coughlin's International Bankers) a kind of self-perpetuating oligarchy, intent on performing or allowing to be performed only one kind of music—the dissonant-contrapuntal style. This is just our old friend Virgil having a good time. For fifteen years now he has been repeating the same thing, as if we didn't know that this same style of modern music, which he supposedly abhors, has served as the perfect foil for the simplicities of Thomson, Sauguet, and Co. Now, as Thomson himself points out, the international style in modern music is rapidly drying up. Everyone is beginning to see the advantages of melodious and harmonious-sounding music. That old gag about the modern-music style is in for some serious revision.

One thing is sure. It will be a long time before there is another book on music as fascinating as this one. Unless Thomson himself can be persuaded to write it.

Schönberg and His School (1949)

RENE LEIBOWITZ, Polish-born composer living in
Paris, himself a student of Schönberg and Webern, is the
latest, and in some ways the most formidable, champion
the Schönberg school has yet had. No serious musician
denies the historical importance of Schönberg's contribution, nor the fact that all contemporary music, directly or
indirectly, owes something to his daring. But to arrive at a
conclusive judgment as to the merits of Schönberg's most
characteristic compositions, as well as those of his pupils,
Alban Berg and Anton Webern, is hardly possible as yet,
because of the infrequent performances their works
are given.* In the meantime the argument continues hotly
in musical and intellectual circles.

To get the most out of this book, one must be prepared to ignore the intensely dogmatic tone of the author.
Leibowitz is the born disciple, with a proselytizing fervor

---

* It is remarkable to note how much music of the Schonberg school has
become readily available on records in the past decade.

seldom encountered in musical treatises. His invective seems deliberately designed to provoke the reader; it works for a while, but in the end is merely wearying, since it has nothing to do, really, with the purpose of the book, which is to make clear the significance of the Schönberg movement.

The thesis might be stated in this way: the essential core of Western music in the last thousand years has been its polyphonic structure. The fact that we, in our music, hear independent melodic lines sounded simultaneously (polyphony) separates our music from that of all other peoples, and gives it its special glory. Unfortunately (according to Leibowitz), simultaneously heard melodies tend to form chords that gradually take on a life of their own as harmony. At first in the modal system and later in the tonal system, harmony pre-empted the place of counterpoint. Melodies were no longer free to move outside their harmonic framework. This hegemony of harmony could not be destroyed until the tonal system itself was destroyed.

It was Wagner who precipitated the suspension of tonality through continual chromatic modulation, and Schönberg who first bravely dispensed with all feeling for tonal centers, thereby freeing polyphony from its harmonic fetters. It was then necessary to organize the new world of atonal sound, which Schönberg proceeded to do with the creation of his compositions written in the twelve-tone system.

The rest of the book is devoted to a brief analysis

of each of the master's works and those of his followers, Berg and Webern. Nowhere in his book does the author speak of the special world—Vienna at the turn of the century—that so strongly influenced the aesthetic ideals of the music of Schönberg and his school. The declining romanticism of that period, with its tense emotionality and its love of complexities, powerfully influenced the new revolutionary music. Its principal adherents, even today, are those who feel a natural affinity with the language of an exaggerated romanticism.*

Leaving aside their specific expressive connotations, Schönberg's innovations posit certain fundamental theoretical problems. Has the tonal system really been exhausted and should it be abandoned or are there still hidden resources to be tapped? Must music always be based on themes, or can we envisage a new athematic music? Isn't it time to find a new way of organizing musical structure based on entirely new principles?

It is one of the ironies of the twelve-tone system that its supporters should be so anxious to prove that they are in the main line of musical tradition. Leibowitz in particular grovels before tradition in a way that is most unsympathetic to the American mind. Especially since this tradition-drenched music actually makes a bewilderingly untraditional impression on the uninitiated listener.

Similarly the author makes a kind of fetish out of musical logic. Faithful to his Central European training, he holds before us the ideal of a music in which there is

---

* No longer a true statement of the musical situation.

"not a single note or figuration which does not result from the development and variation of the basic motive." But isn't it ironic that it should be just this music, of an undeniable ingenuity in note-for-note logic, that appears to have no inevitability of flow for the unprejudiced ear?

In the name of logic Leibowitz contends that only the music of twelve-tone composers can be considered truly representative of our time. Perhaps. But then what are we to do with triflers like Stravinsky and Satie—abandon them for the good of our musical souls? As an antidote to so much method I suggest that the author relax long enough to contemplate the charms of the unanalyzable and the non-systematic, which, after all, is what makes music an art and not a science.

For this reader the chapters devoted to the music of Anton Webern were the most absorbing. Here one finds material nowhere else available in English. Whatever the purely musical quality of his music may prove to be, it makes clear that Webern undoubtedly possessed one of the most original musical minds of our century, and that he carried the implications of the twelve-tone system closest to their inevitable conclusion.

In spite of its fanatical tone and dense prose style this is an important book for all those professionals who want an authoritative analysis of the workings of the Schönberg system. I doubt whether it can be of much use to the musical layman. It has been faithfully translated by Miss Dika Newlin, herself an American devotee of the master's school.

The Life and Music of Bartók (1953)

COMPOSER, CRITIC, AND HEAD of the Composition Department at the University of Southern California, Halsey Stevens has written the first full-length study of Béla Bartók to be published in English. Bartók presents an absorbing task for any biographer. He was a major figure in the contemporary musical scene with a personality not easily fathomable. And his body of work provides the kind of complex material a professional musician loves to explore.

Being himself a composer, Mr. Stevens naturally is concerned more with the work than with the life of the composer. There is no reason to regret this, except that the appeal of his book is thus limited. Professional musicians will find the sober and erudite analyses of musical textures highly interesting; others will have to await a more Boswellian biographer.

The first third of the book relates in straightforward fashion the main facts of Bartók's life. There is no attempt to probe the special fascination of the Bartókian temperament: the shyness and personal reticence that hid an indomitably independent spirit; the freedom of the inspired artist held in check by an almost pedantic self-discipline. Nor does Mr. Stevens dwell upon another curious aspect of the Bartók story: why it was that his death in 1945 seemed to touch off an enormous increase in the performances of his works. Most affecting is the unadorned recital of Bartók's illnesses and financial difficulties during his last years in American exile. Excerpts from the composer's letters in this section reveal him in the unsuspected role of a delightful correspondent.

The rest of the book is given over to a careful examination of every composition Bartók ever wrote, divided according to category. In each instance the author knows what he thinks and states it persuasively. He seems to have had in mind a reference text, most useful to those with the musical score readily at hand. This emphasis on textual exposition engenders a thesis-like atmosphere at times, and Mr. Stevens is not averse to throwing in an occasional term that glares at one from the page through its unfamiliarity (the "crasis" of the piano, the "dioristic" details of traditional forms).

Embedded in the factual descriptive matter are many acute and cogent observations regarding Bartók's musical mentality and style that the ordinary music-lover would find illuminating, if only they were written into a more "normal" context. As it is, he is unlikely ever to find them at all, and that's a pity.

Mr. Stevens is at his best when he is most outspoken —when he has a special point to plead. He is particularly eloquent on the subject of Bartók's finest achievement, the six string quartets. Some of his most perceptive writing will be found in that chapter, especially his enthusiasm for the more recondite examples of the form—Quartets Nos. 3 and 4. He can be sharply critical also, and rightly so, it would seem, as in the case of the posthumously reconstructed *Concerto for Viola*, whose defects he clearly exposes.

As was to be expected, the book amply demonstrates the close connection between Bartók's musical manner and his lifelong preoccupation with Hungarian folk-song sources and those of adjoining nationalities. Despite earlier examples of musical nationalism in the work of Glinka, Smetana, and Grieg, it was left for Bartók to show in a definitive way that a simple folk song did not necessarily imply a simple harmonic setting based on conventional harmonies. Having wedded folk song to modern harmony, the composer then successfully incorporated native musical materials into extended musical forms. And in the final metamorphosis, as Mr. Stevens phrases it, Bartók "employs neither folk melodies nor imitations of folk melodies, but absorbs their essence in such a way that it pervades his music."

Mr. Stevens is not an impressionist critic; he is not satisfied until he pin-points these essences as themes, motives, rhythms, and scale structures. He is particularly keen in writing of Bartók's handling of the two- or three-note motive. These, Mr. Stevens writes, are "in a continuous state of regeneration. They grow organically; they proliferate; the evolutionary process is kinetic . . . the line between reason and intuition is never sharply defined, but the compact thematic logic cannot be denied."

Mr. Stevens' book does credit to American musical scholarship. It makes one want to rehear the Bartók works in the light of what the author has found in them. That is praise indeed for any book on music.

SECTION FOUR

Occasional Pieces

1. "ARE MY EARS ON WRONG?": A POLEMIC*

MUSICAL COMPOSITION during the first half of our century was vigorously alive partly because of the amount of controversy it was able to arouse. As the century advanced the noise of battle receded until by now we had reluctantly come to assume that the good fight for the acceptance of modern music was over. It was welcome news, therefore, to hear that a rear-guard attack was about to be launched from what used to be a main source of opposition: the professional music critic. It looked as if we were in for some old-fashioned fisticuffs, but the nature of the attack soured our expectations. The trouble is that,

* In 1955, Henry Pleasants, music critic, published a book entitled *The Agony of Modern Music*, in which he attacked the writers of serious music and hailed the genius of the jazz composer. The New York *Times Magazine* invited Mr. Pleasants to sum up the argument of his book and asked me to present the case for the defense. This is my first and only essay in musical polemics.

according to his analysis, Henry Pleasants is pummeling nothing but a carcass.

He contends that so-called classical music is bankrupt in our age—the old forms of symphony and concerto and opera are exhausted, all our vaunted innovations are old hat, and the serious composer is obsolete. The present-day writer of serious music is held up to view as a sort of musical parvenu, incapable of earning a living through musical composition, skulking about the concert halls for musical crumbs, sought after by none, desperately trying to convince himself that he is rightful heir to the heritage of the masters, and deluding public and critics alike into conferring upon him a spurious respectability for "culture's" sake. The clear implication is that the best we can do is to lie down and die.

But if all is lost for us, the serious composers, music itself goes on, Mr. Pleasants tells us. It is *vox populi*, as expressed at the box office, that shows the way. Fearlessly and logically pursuing his argument to its absurd conclusion, he asserts that the stream of Western musical culture continues triumphantly in the music of our popular composers. "Jazz is modern music—and nothing else is." So ends the most confused book on music ever issued in America.

The question arises as to whether it serves any purpose to attempt a defense of serious contemporary music. I hold to the simple proposition that the only way to comprehend a "difficult" piece of abstract sculpture is to keep looking at it, and the only way to understand "difficult" modern music is to keep listening to it. (Not all of it is difficult listening, by the way.) For that reason it seems basically useless to explain the accomplishments of present-day music to people who are incapable of getting any excitement out of it.

If you hear this music and fail to realize that it has added a new dimension to Western musical art, that it has a power and tension and expressiveness typically twentieth-century in quality, that it has overcome the rhythmic inhibitions of the nineteenth century and added complexes of chordal progressions never before conceived, that it has invented subtle or brash combinations of hitherto-unheard timbres, that it offers new structural principles that open up vistas for the future—I say, if your pulse remains steady at the contemplation of all this and if listening to it does not add up to a fresh and different musical experience for you, then any defense of mine, or of anybody else, can be of no use whatsoever.

The plain fact is that the composer of our century has earned the right to be considered a master of new sonorous images. Because of him music behaves differently, its textures are different—more crowded or more spacious, it sings differently, it rears itself more suddenly and plunges more precipitously. It even stops differently. But it shares with older music the expression of basic human emotions, even though at times it may seem more painful, more nostalgic, more obscure, more hectic, more sarcastic. Whatever else it may be, it is the voice of our own age and in that sense it needs no apology.

This is the music we are told nobody likes. But let's take a closer look at "nobody." There is general agreement that new multitudes have come to serious music listening in the past two or three decades. Now we are faced with a situation long familiar in the literary world; namely, the need to differentiate clearly among the various publics available to the writer. No publisher of an author-philosopher like Whitehead would expect him to reach the enormous public of a novelist like Hemingway. Ought we then to say "nobody" reads Whitehead?

In music we have failed to make distinctions among lovers of serious works. Thus the philosophical music of Charles Ives is discussed as if it were meant to appeal to the same audience reached by music of the Khachaturian type. To say that Ives, or any similar composer, has "no audience" is like saying that Whitehead has no audience. He has, through the nature of his work, a smaller but no less enthusiastic audience—and one that in the long view may mean more to the art of music than the "big" audience will.

Moreover, if one takes the whole free world into account, there is a small but growing public for new music in every country. These people are not to be found in the convention-ridden concert halls but in the record shops as independent collectors, or as listeners to new music, recorded or otherwise, broadcast over the air. The long-play record catalogues bear interesting testimony concerning contemporary musical taste. In January 1950 they listed ten LP recordings by Béla Bartók; five years later, fifty Bartók works were available. Schönberg, Stravinsky, Hindemith, Milhaud—all show proportionate gains. If nobody likes modern music, why do the record makers foolishly continue to issue it?

Nevertheless, it is quite true that a serious problem remains with regard to the live performance of unfamiliar modern music for the "big" public. Analogies here are closer to the theater than the book world. Our problem in music arises from the fact that Ives and Khachaturian must be "sold" to the same public at the same box office at the same time. The impresarios have a simple solution: remove the Ives.

Sponsors and trustees repeatedly tell us that unfamiliar music spells losses. But isn't it ironic that those who are responsible for artistic policy at the Metropolitan Opera House or the New York Philharmonic Orchestra must watch the box office like the lowliest moneygrubber on Broadway?

What we need in music is people with the vision of those who founded the Museum of Modern Art twenty-five years ago, people willing to spend for the sake of the future of art and the cultural health of the community. If new music is "poison at the box office," it is the responsibility of those who direct our cultural organizations to find funds sufficient to counteract this poison. Otherwise conductors and performers will gradually become nothing more than mummified guardians of a musical museum, while composers look for other outlets for their creative energies.

One of the more fanciful notions of the Pleasants book is the idea that music that does not pay its way is to give place to music that does—namely, jazz. The juxtaposition of "jazz" and "classical" has been going on for a long time now. I can remember it as an amusing vaudeville act when I was a boy. No one took it seriously then and there is no reason why it should be taken seriously now.

Certainly what our popular composers have accomplished is a source of pride to all of us. Anyone who has heard American jazz played for an audience in a foreign country, as I have, can testify to its enormous appeal. But to imagine that serious music is endangered by the wide acceptance of our popular music, or that one may be substituted for the other, is to be utterly naïve as to comparative musical values.

Why are these two categories of music incommensurable? Two reasons must suffice here: the character and quality of the emotion aroused, and the relation of length to significance. To take the latter first: equating a thirty-minute symphony with a three-minute song is like equating a five-act play with an eight-line poem. An art like music, if successfully carried out, adds significance through its playing time, since the large conception that is implicit in a long work forces the creator to grapple with problems of organization and development and variety that can rightfully be applied to only important materials. An inspired eight-line poem is worth more than a poorly conceived five-act play, to be sure, but this does not change the basic principle involved.

Can we then equate a two-page popular composition with one of similar length by Scarlatti or Prokofieff? Here the scale is the same but the emotional substance is likely to be different. Artistic substance is admittedly a matter one can argue endlessly. A good blues song may be a sincerely felt and moving expression, but the substance of the emotion aroused is generally less affecting than that awakened by a moving and sincerely felt spiritual, for example.

There is no way of proving this except through consensus. Similarly, there is no way of proving that a Scarlatti piano piece is better than a piece of popular music except to point out that it has a more subtle musical invention and formal organization and means more because it didn't come off the top of the composer's mind and isn't easily forgotten.

It is nevertheless not at all unlikely that a modern Scarlatti might turn to jazz as a legitimate form of expression. As a matter of fact, the newer forms of progressive jazz promise composers of the liveliest imagination. But it is undeniable that this type of jazz composer is well aware of and helps himself to devices of the serious modern composer, and more often than not turns out to be a pupil of one. Also jazz composers of this caliber meet with the same sort of opposition from the "big" public as their counterparts in the serious field.

Whatever form of new music is contemplated, one

thing is certain: without generosity of spirit one can understand nothing. Without openness, warmth, goodwill, the lending of one's ears, nothing new in music can possibly reach us.

Charles Ives, ruminating on why it was his music seemed to "upset people," ruefully asked himself: "Are my ears on wrong?" It isn't a bad idea for the composer to take an occasional look in the mirror. But the mirror must not be one of those penny-arcade distortion affairs that Mr. Pleasants has set up.

2. INTERPRETERS
AND NEW MUSIC*

A VISITING COMPOSER like myself, settled in May-
fair for a dozen weeks goes program-shopping more
or less as the typical American tourist goes window-
shopping. No tourist can hope to buy everything—just as I
have no intention of hearing everything—but it is always
of interest to know what is being offered in the music
emporiums of a world center.

One is naturally on the lookout for musical fare not
obtainable at home. My own peering into London's programs of the recent past and those to come has left me
rather disgruntled: what is being offered, in the main, is
a rehash of more of the same. I don't wish to appear too
surprised: something of the sort, I suppose, was to be
expected. Why? Because the condition is world-wide;

* Reprinted from the music page of the London *Sunday Times*, October
12, 1958.

whether one is in Buenos Aires or Tel-Aviv or New Orleans, audiences are usually offered "more of the same." One signal difference is that London seems to have contracted the more-of-the-same disease in a more virulent form than is evident elsewhere.

There is no need to paint the picture blacker than it is. I realize that there are notable exceptions in evenings such as the BBC's all-Monteverdi program or the London Philharmonic Orchestra's Twentieth Century series. (The latter, I was pleased to see, attracted a large and enthusiastic public at its opening concert.) But these only point up the all-pervading conventionality of the run-of-the-mill concert program. In such surroundings Debussy and Ravel look like ultramodernists.

The musical life of a great city is a complex and often puzzling affair. A mere visitor can hardly hope to say who or what is responsible for the present unhappy situation. (It may even be ungracious of me to bring the matter up at all.) But in so far as the appalling sameness of repertoire is a universal problem it bears examination by any serious musician. Other commentators have put the blame in various quarters: the money-harassed impresarios, the timid or unimaginative program directors; and, of course, that simple soul, the uninformed music-lover, has also been the subject of considerable invective.

Apart from every other consideration I have often wondered about the effect of all this on the performing artist, without whose intervention nothing can be heard. It is almost inconceivable for a composer to imagine what it must be like to confine one's musical activity to the endless repetition of the same famous pieces by the same famous composers, season after season, year after year. To us these artists seem trapped: they spend their lives in sonic strait-jackets, manufactured in their despite by the master composers. How do they react to their sorry state? Some appear to accept the inevitable; others are so inured to their condition they hardly realize what has happened to them; still others—especially ensemble musicians who must play the music set before them—harbor their frustrations in silence.

Every composer has had occasion to think about what he might say or do to reawaken these musicians to a sense of responsibility to the art they serve, to reanimate their interest in the whole corpus of musical literature, old and new. What, after all, is the responsibility of the performer to the art of music? Isn't it to keep music fully alive, renewed, refreshed? And how is that to be accomplished if the interpreter fails us?

One important touchstone of the performer's sense of responsibility is his relationship with the music of his own time. Many of them, I know, have no relation of any kind. This is particularly true of many of the great virtuoso performers, whose names can easily be inserted by my readers. It is my impression that 75 per cent of the performers now before the public have lost all contact with the music of their living contemporaries. Each one of them has a bad conscience in this matter, and with cause. Not having kept abreast of today's music, they are positively frightened of it. And yet they need such music to relieve the stylistic monotony of their programs. I have never known a public concert of a variegated make-up that wasn't enlivened by ten minutes of controversial music. Even those who are sure to hate it are given something to talk about. Involvement in contemporary music aids the interpreter in another significant way. To my mind no one can adequately interpret the classics of the past without hearing them through the ears of the present. To play or conduct Beethoven's *scherzi* in a contemporary spirit, you must feel at home with Stravinskian rhythms. And I can even recommend familiarity with the rhythms of American jazz for those who want to play Couperin.

Not all famous performers are to be reproached with their neglect of the living composer. In the distant past Artur Rubinstein was acclaimed for his sponsorship of the music of Villa-Lobos, and Sir Thomas Beecham for his persistent championing of the music of Delius. Perhaps the most outstanding example in recent times was the effective battle fought by Serge Koussevitzky in introducing a whole generation of American composers to the United States public. I know at first hand of the Russian conductor's efforts on behalf of the newer composers, having been one of his principal beneficiaries. It was a lesson in leadership to observe how, over a period of twenty-five years, Koussevitzky used every possible tactic to win over his listeners (and his orchestra) to a cause he passionately believed in.

Apathy in the making of programs—giving the public

what it wants and nothing but what it wants—leads to the complete stagnation of music as an art. Can anyone seriously maintain that that is all that lies ahead? In some way, not clear to me as yet, we must persuade the interpreter to take a hand in the making of musical history by letting us hear the full sonorous range of music's past and present.

3. THE DILEMMA OF OUR SYMPHONY ORCHESTRAS*

SOMETHING IS STRANGELY AMISS in the orchestral world of today. It is natural that we be concerned, for our symphony orchestras are without question the most important and vital musical medium in the country. The symphony orchestra is at the same time the nerve center of any musical community and the composer's favorite medium. Most musical creators have a rather sentimental feeling about symphony orchestras. To a composer, anybody that has anything to do with an orchestra has a certain glamour, all the way from the conductor to the janitor of the auditorium. Since our future as composers is very largely bound up with the symphonic medium, we are naturally deeply concerned with its present situation and future outlook.

* Address delivered at the Providence, R.I., convention of the American Symphony Orchestra League in June 1956.

Composers are generally convinced that if the present policies of most orchestras continue as they now exist, then we are all headed for some kind of dead-end. By and large our symphony orchestras have no real long-range program policy. They operate from week to week, from season to season, as if they were improvising their whole program. If they get by in any one season they are happy. If they do not get by (if there is a deficit, that is), they are sad. But that is not the way the composer sees the problem. To him the problem exists even when any particular orchestra plays to full houses and has no deficit. What we must all do is to take a larger view.

The audience, after all, is the central factor in this situation. What music the audience hears depends largely on those who control programming—whether it be the conductor, the manager, the board of trustees, the ladies auxiliary committee, or whoever. Those responsible have the double task of satisfying the audience and providing a forward-looking, long-range program policy. But if we study typical programs today, what do we find? We find programs that are limited in scope, repetitious in content, and therefore unexciting. Present programming tends to stultify and mummify our musical public. Under such conditions we composers are strongly tempted to ask: What are you doing to our audiences? Frankly, we have very little confidence when we bring our pieces before such audiences. Often we sense that the audience that listens to us is not the right audience for our music. Why? Because they have not been musically nurtured and fed properly, with a resultant vitamin lack of musical understanding.

The key to a healthy orchestral future is now, as it always has been, the quality and balance of its program make-up. This has been pointed out many times, with little or no result. No other art shows a similar imbalance between old and new works presented. No other art attempts to live so exclusively on works of the past. This may provide a temporary solution but it builds to no future, for no live art can exist forever on a diet of past glories alone.

The situation as it now exists is by no means a local one. It is also typical of what goes on in other countries. Recently the French composer Henri Dutilleux provided graphic illustration as to the deteriorating conditions in Parisian program making. He chose four famous French orchestras in Paris and compared the number of works by living French composers performed by these same orchestras in the month of January 1925, 1935, and 1955. Here is what he found: in January 1925, 31 works were played by living Frenchmen; in January 1935, 17 works; and in January 1955, only 4 works.

We in America can supply analogous statistics. The New York Philharmonic Symphony Society has a better-than-average reputation as a purveyor of new works. And yet here is the record of works by living American composers performed during the four seasons 1950–51 through 1953–54.*

* Since the advent of the American conductor Leonard Bernstein as musical director, these figures have improved, but they remain true nevertheless for the average American orchestra.

Season	Total number of works performed	Number of works by living Americans
1950–51	155	9
1951–52	143	9
1952–53	159	5
1953–54	176	11

Despite the generally recognized rise in American creative vigor in the symphonic field, no comparable rise in the number of performances is discernible. On the contrary, statistics prove that we continue to drag our feet in a continuance of the status quo. The National Music Council has drawn up comparative figures that show the percentage of performed works by native American composers to have remained the same in two seasons fifteen years apart: 8 per cent in 1939, and 8 per cent in 1954, despite the fact that double the number of works were performed in 1954. More American music had been played, but the percentage of all works played had remained the same.

America prides itself on progress. But these figures do not speak well for what is going on. Rather they indicate a shocking lack of live interest and civic pride in the accomplishments and future of our American music. The effect of all this on the developing composer is naturally very grave. A young composer simply cannot produce the best he is capable of in so unpromising an environment. In the last five years I can think of no single American composer under the age of thirty who has been nurtured or encouraged in the United States because of the efforts of one of our leading symphony orchestras. More and more our organizations are depending on well-known American names to fill out their quota of native music. Less and less are they seeking out and introducing completely unknown names of real promise. Unless our symphonic organizations take on this responsibility, they are not entirely fulfilling their cultural task. Worse still, they are obstructing the flowering of one of our most significant national assets, the gifted young composer.

It seems to me that in doing little or nothing to stimulate new talent our symphony societies show surprisingly limited business acumen. If a commercial enterprise ran its affairs with so small a regard for its future welfare, stockholders would soon melt away. Most big firms invest funds with an eye to what their business is headed for ten years hence. Why shouldn't that attitude also apply in the symphonic field? Isn't it ironic that this apparent lack of planned interest in the future of our native school should come at a time when we have more composers writing works that are demonstrably better in quality than ever before in our musical history.

An instructive comparison may be made by taking note of what transpires in recorded music as regards native composition. David Hall reports that we now have some five hundred works by American composers available on long-play records. I have always been astonished by the seeming unconcern of those in the concert field as to what goes on in the record market. Why shouldn't symphony management occasionally find out what people are buying in the record shops? These record buyers interest composers very much because they are making up their own minds as to what it is they prefer to hear. In the case of more than one recording I can report that despite excellent sales reports this clear show of interest was absolutely unreflected in the concert world. As long as the concert hall is unresponsive in this matter of listening tastes, people who buy records are not going to be persuaded to enter the concert hall. If this continues, a widening split will become increasingly evident between those who are content to listen passively at concerts and those who demonstrate a passionate interest in the music they want to hear.

Here and now we cannot hope to do more than stimulate discussion of these vital matters. Perhaps I can summarize my thought by making a few specific suggestions:

1. A system of checks and balances should be instituted so that each orchestra guarantee itself adequate variety in programs throughout a season chosen from different categories of the musical repertoire.

2. Every concert should deliberately have an element challenging to an audience, so as to counteract conventional attitudes in music response.

3. Seeking out and developing new talent in orchestral writing should be made a permanent feature of basic policy.

4. SHOP TALK: ON THE
NOTATION OF RHYTHM

IN A RECENT ARTICLE in *Modern Music*, Marcelle de Manziarly demonstrated that there exist two different kinds of rhythm in music of a more sophisticated nature; namely, the rhythm one hears, and the rhythm one hears and sees. The ear alone, without the aid of the eye, can distinguish only elementary types, made up of strong and weak beats, evenly or unevenly grouped together, heard singly or in combinations. In a simple waltz or march the ear easily grasps what the mental eye sees. But just as the trained musician occasionally likes to follow from score—perhaps in order to more clearly extricate the inner voices from the general musical texture, so the eye helps to appreciate rhythmic subtleties that the ear cannot take in. This distinction should be stressed more than it has been.

It is a distinction that becomes crucial in the noting

Occasional Pieces

down of certain so-called modern rhythms—rhythms that present a technical problem both to the composer himself and to his executant.*

Most of us were brought up in the rhythmic tradition of the nineteenth century, which took for granted the equal division of metrical units. Countless pupils were taught that four quarter notes: ♩♩♩♩ indicate accents on beats one and three: <u>1</u>-2-<u>3</u>-4 ; and that when these were subdivided, the smaller units would always be equal divisions, thus: ♫ ♫ ♫ ♫ .   Trouble began when composers became fascinated with the rhythmic possibilities resulting from the combination of unequal units of twos and threes: ♫ ♫♫ or ♫♫ ♫ . Basically a large proportion of modern rhythms may be said to derive from that formula.

If you happen to be the type of composer who hears successions of two and three eighth-note groupings, you are likely to find yourself writing down combinations like this: |⅜ ♫ ♫♫ |⅝ ♫ ♫♫ ♫♫ |⅞ ♫♫ ♫ ♫ |²⁄₈ ♫ |³⁄₈ ♫♫ |

Here you have the by-now-familiar groups of unequal metrical units that strike terror in the hearts of performers, particularly conductors—who know in advance the struggles in store for them when these rhythmic complexes are brought to rehearsal.

The harassed executant is quick to point out that in his opinion the composer was inventing unnecessary com-

---

* In the past decade the serialization of rhythmic units by the dodecaphonic school of composers has greatly complicated the problem as set forth here.

274

plications in the notating of his rhythms. The argument goes something like this: In writing down groupings of 5/8–8/8–7/8–3/8, or any similar "odd" combination, you are proceeding on the assumption that all strong beats coincide with the first beat of each measure. In other words, you are making rhythm and meter synonymous, a practice in much nineteenth-century music. Walter Piston put the case well for the executant when he wrote:

"The overemphasis on the musical significance of the barline and the attempt to make meter and rhythm synonymous should perhaps be laid to the influence of Stravinsky and Bartók. After the *Sacre* our young composers fell under a tyranny of the bar measure quite as strict as that which held sway during the nineteenth century, forgetting that the barline in music is only a convenience for keeping time and that it indicates rhythmic stress only by accident and coincidence."

If that is true—if the bar-line is not to be taken as indicative of a strong beat—then our rhythm of:

(Version 1)
might just as well be noted down as:

(Version 2)
Theoretically, whichever way the rhythm is notated (always assuming that accents have been added), the effect on the ear should be the same.

That would seem to settle the question. But actually there are two schools of thought in this matter. The younger and more progressive type of interpreter will tell you that, despite its difficulty, he prefers Version 1 to Version 2. He insists that executants must be taught to play unequal rhythmic units with the same natural ease that they play a simple ternary rhythm. He claims further that the two versions do not in reality sound precisely the same to the listening ear. A subtle difference will be felt as between one version and the other.

It seems to me true that, from the standpoint of the individual performer who plays without a conductor, both versions should be equally assimilable. The considerable advantage of Version 1 is that it looks the way it sounds. But for ensemble playing under the baton of a leader, experience has taught me that Version 2 is preferred by the majority of instrumentalists and conductors. It is not always technically easy to ignore the bar-line, as one must in playing Version 2, placing the accents where they are indicated. But once the rhythm is well learned it is easy to reproduce; while Version 1, even when thoroughly rehearsed, is easy to forget.

One of the difficulties of trying to settle this matter of rhythmic notation once and for all arises from the fact that no one example can be made to stand for all possible rhythmic problems. Each separate instance must be decided on its own merit. For example, speaking generally, it would seem foolish to force a basic rhythm of 7/8, which consistently remains 7/8 throughout a piece or section of a piece, into a strait-jacket of 3/4 or 4/4 merely for the sake of a more conventional regularity. There are other instances where the addition of an extra eighth or sixteenth note to an otherwise regular rhythmic scheme will cause notational upsets. These are sometimes unavoidable, and can be accounted for only by the interpolation of an occasional uneven measure. Common sense dictates the use of the metrically regular bar-line whenever the actual rhythms are persistently irregular. These are the rhythms that have to be simplified, at least for the present, until executants catch up with the complex rhythmic imagination of the present-day composer.

Mademoiselle de Manziarly goes so far as to suggest that some of the contemporary works in the standard repertory might well be renovated along these simplified lines. She adds: "I wonder if this would have been possible at the time they were written. The new world of rhythm they represented was unfamiliar; it needed to be firmly underlined by placing the beginning of each segment of phrase on the strong beat, regardless of the asymmetric succession of unequal measures." Whatever men like Bartók and Stravinsky might say to this rebarring proposal, it is evident that their recent works usually show a more normal notation. Works that are polyrhythmic by nature almost force this solution, since the presence of independent strong beats in different voices cannot possibly be adequately represented by a single bar-line.

Let us grant, then, the case of the performing artist who prefers a regular metric division in music, provided that the sense of the non-coinciding rhythm is clear. But is it invariably crystal-clear? Do we always know when the bar-line is there merely for convenience (that is, to be

Occasional Pieces

disregarded) and when it is there as an indication of rhythmic stress (to be taken into account)? In theory the musical sense of the line should tell us what the real rhythm is. But in practice we find composers inventing little subterfuges for keeping the strong beat clear of the bar-line. Here are a few examples of solutions adopted by some well-known composers:

Milhaud

Stravinsky

Bartók

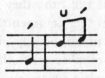

Schönberg

or common practice

This would seem to show that the use of accents, placed to indicate qualitative rhythm, is insufficient. It is

bar-line as here, or as we would, to the left (1st. (A.)

2 7 8

common knowledge that an accent, taken by itself, is an unsubtle sign. Notes have light, strong, and medium accents. There are accents on up-beats as well as down-beats. There are accents that even allow the bar-line to be "felt." All these are now symbolized by the simple sign>. (Sheer desperation must have mothered the addition of the *sforzato* sign for very strong accents.) It is obvious that we badly need an enlarged system of musical symbols to serve our greater rhythmic complexities.

It seems unlikely, however, that a scientifically exact scheme of rhythmic notation will ever be devised. Much of the delicate rhythmic variety we are accustomed to hearing in first-rate performances is simply not written down by the composer—could not be written down in our present system of notation. A certain rhythmic freedom seems to be an integral part of our Western musical tradition. Nevertheless, without attempting the impossible, it certainly appears highly desirable that some more satisfactory method than our present one be devised to account for rhythmic subtleties that don't "get across" to the interpreter in our old fashioned notational system.

In my opinion composers would do well to notate their music so that, as far as possible, it looks the way it sounds. If the work is written for solo performer there is usually no need for tampering further with the rhythm. If, however, more than one player is involved, and especially in the case of orchestral works, a rearrangement of rhythmic barring may be necessary.† The more rhythmically sophisticated conductors will not think so, but performances are more likely to materialize.

† For the student it may be interesting to compare the two different barrings of my *El Salón México* as they appear in the published versions for orchestra and for solo piano.

Music Titles in
The Norton Library

Norton Books in Music

Norton / Haydn Society Records

A TREASURY OF EARLY MUSIC

Four 12-inch 33⅓ RPM long-play records to supplement Parrish's *A Treasury of Early Music*. Monaural and Stereophonic.

Parrish's *A Treasury of Early Music*. Monaural and Stereo.

Record 1   *Music of the Middle Ages*
Examples 1 through 12

Record 2   *Music of the Ars Nova and the Renaissance*
Examples 13 through 28

Record 3   *Music of the Renaissance and Baroque*
Examples 29 through 41

Record 4   *Music of the Baroque*
Examples 42 through 50

MASTERPIECES OF MUSIC BEFORE 1750

Three 12-inch 33⅓ RPM long-play records to supplement Parrish and Ohl, *Masterpieces of Music Before 1750*. Monaural.

Record 1   *Gregorian Chant to the 16th Century*
Examples 1 through 22

Record 2   *The 16th and 17th Centuries*
Examples 23 through 36

Record 3   *The 17th and 18th Centuries*
Examples 37 through 50